CROS

WITH

CROSS TRAIN
WITH TAI CHI

A BALANCED APPROACH TO IMPROVING
YOUR SPORTS PERFORMANCE,
HEALTH AND OVERALL WELLBEING

MIKE TAYLOR

Copyright @ Mike Taylor (2017)
Published by Mike Taylor Publishing

First Edition (2017)

All rights reserved. No part of this publication, including illustrations, may be reproduced or transmitted in any form or by any means, mechanical or electronic, including photocopying, recording, or by any information storage and retrieval system, or transmitted by email without the prior permission in writing of the Author/publisher.

www.taichicrosstraining.com

eBook ISBN: 978-0-9957065-0-7
Paperback ISBN: 978-0-9957065-1-4

Cover Design: Rick Holland, Vision Press
Interior Design: Dean Fetzer at GunBoss.com

Disclaimer

While all attempts have been made to verify the information provided in this publication, neither the author nor the publisher assumes any responsibility for errors, omissions, or contrary interpretations of the subject matter herein.

The author and publisher of this book are not responsible in any manner whatsoever for any injury that may result from practicing the techniques and/or following the instructions given within. Since the physical activities herein may be too strenuous in nature for some readers to engage in safely, it is essential that a physician is consulted prior to training.

The views expressed are those of the author and should not be taken as expert instruction or commands. The reader is responsible for his or her own actions.

Contents

Acknowledgements	**i**
1. Introduction	**1**
1.1 Why Cross Train?	*4*
1.2 Benefits of Cross Training with Tai Chi	*9*
1.3 What's in the Book?	*13*
2. Cross Training With Tai Chi	**17**
2.1 An Introduction to Tai Chi	*17*
2.2 What is Qi?	*23*
2.3 Mind/Body Integration	*25*
2.4 Tai Chi Relaxation and Breathing	*33*
2.5 Opening Neuromuscular Pathways	*36*
2.6 Tai Chi for Sports	*39*
2.7 Why do we need to balance our Energy?	*56*
3. Mind-Body Integration for Peak Performance	**59**
3.1 Sports Science and Sports Psychology	*59*
3.2 Stress and Mindfulness	*63*
3.3 Keeping your Mind Calm with Tai Chi	*65*
3.4 Tai Chi Essential Principles	*66*
3.5 In the Zone	*74*

4. A Tai Chi Training Program   77

4.1 Face-to-Face or Online Course?   *77*

4.2 An Example Training Program   *84*

4.3 A Typical Training Course   *85*

5. How Do I know it's Working?   91

5.1 Deliberate Practice and Managing your Expectations   *91*

5.2 Tracking Progress   *98*

5.3 Is it Working?   *101*

5.4 Next Steps   *109*

6. Resources   111

About the Author   115

Acknowledgements

My deepest thanks go to the following people who contributed directly or indirectly, to this book.

My wife Liz, for her everlasting love, support, and guidance, not only throughout the process of writing this book but also for supporting me in my quest to learn and deepen my Tai Chi Chuan knowledge and skills over the last 18 years.

To my teacher Grandmaster Yang Jun – Traditional Yang family Tai Chi Chuan lineage holder and one of China's most respected and senior judges. Without Grandmaster Yang's excellent teaching, dedication and commitment I would not have travelled so far on my Tai Chi journey.

To Therese Teo Mei Mei – Disciple of Grandmaster Yang ZhenDuo (4th generation lineage holder). For introducing me to the wonderful art of Yang family Tai Chi Chuan, and continuing to guide and teach me as I continue my studies.

And, finally to all my fellow Tai Chi brothers and sisters around the world, without their support and dedication, the International Yang family Tai Chi Chuan Association would not have been able to spread the excellence of Tai Chi throughout the world.

1. Introduction

This book is very different to 99% of the cross training books written to date. Most of the information in books produced today focus on individual cross training exercises that develop muscular strength or improve cardiovascular fitness. This book however, shows how a completely different, but integrated system of exercise should be considered to help improve an athlete's sports performance, and thereby achieve their performance goals.

Please take a minute or so to review and answer the questions below:

- Are you happy with your current primary sports achievements and performance?

- Are you looking for that something new, or different, to give you that extra edge? And at the same time re-

energise your body, strengthen your immune system, and improve your performance and overall health?

- Are you fed up with the 'same old' exercises and routines?

- Are you undertaking any form of cross training? If so, is your cross training still focused on high intensity cardiovascular or muscle building exercises?

- Could you compliment your primary sports training with a form of cross training that focuses on integrating both the mind and body elements in one coercive system, thereby supporting your development and helping you achieve peak performance?

- Are you feeling there is something missing?

Hopefully, by reviewing and answering the questions above, I've managed to grab your attention and interest so far. If so, please take the next 10 minutes or so to read the rest of this introduction and decide if you're interested in trying out a new approach to cross training, where the focus is on postural awareness, dynamic relaxation and the complete integration of mind and body, rather than continuing with the same old 'no pain no gain' boring muscle building or cardiovascular training!

1. Introduction

The system of exercise I am referring to is Tai Chi Chuan. Some of you may be tempted to stop reading now, as you would normally associate Tai Chi with groups of older people, probably over sixty years of age, practicing strange slow movements in a park. I can hear you saying, 'How can Tai Chi help me, a serious or professional athlete, improve my performance?'

Stay with me and I will take you on a journey to show you that cross training with Tai Chi is an ideal exercise for both younger and older athletes, and greater benefits can be realised if you start your Tai Chi training earlier, ideally in your late teens, twenties, or early thirties.

Tai Chi, as it's most commonly known, is a fully integrated mind and body exercise system that can be safely integrated into your current training schedule to make that extra difference. The difference I am talking about is in strengthening the body's immune system, and improving your performance and overall health.

The art of Tai Chi will help to relieve tension, and reduce the stress and anxiety that comes with pushing yourself to improve or win. Tai Chi promotes a more mindful, focused and relaxed approach to achieving your primary sports goals.

Let's begin by taking a look at why cross training can be instrumental in improving your performance, and why cross training with Tai Chi provides a dynamic and relaxed

Cross Train With Tai Chi

approach to not only performance improvement, but also helps to strengthen your immune system, thereby creating a healthier mind and body.

1.1 Why Cross Train?

The pressure to maintain or improve sports performance is at an all-time high. For example, professional sportsmen and woman are under ever-increasing media focus to deliver and maintain high-level performance in line with their coach's, peers and family expectations.

This is not only true for professional athletes; the amateur athlete can also experience a similar pressure today. Many are extremely serious about their level of performance and achievements, constantly resetting their goals to keep themselves in tip-top condition, motivated, and seeking out small improvements in their performance. In pushing themselves to improve they often push themselves to the limit, where the line between fitness and good health becomes blurred (more about this a little later), and they hope they can stay fit and injury free.

Both professionals and serious amateurs are typically affected by increased stress and anxiety when they don't perform or achieve as expected. This in turn, can lead to problems maintaining performance and focus, both 'on the

1. Introduction

field' and in their daily lives, which in turn can lead to a loss of self-belief and confidence in their ability and cause mental and physical health issues.

What can athletes do to minimise their stresses and strains? One answer is to incorporate cross training into their weekly exercise regime. For example, many athletes, particularly cyclists, runners and endurance athletes add weight training or additional cardiovascular type training to their exercise programs. However, these types of exercises are still about pumping more blood around the body, building muscular strength and improving stamina, where a more effective approach is to select another form of exercise where the body and mind are not put under even more stress.

Some athletes practice or try out mind related exercises, where the focus is on clearing and calming the mind when they find themselves in a pressurised or stressful situation, for example, serving for the set or match in Tennis or standing at the first Tee in Golf. This type of training is often approached through the field of Sports Psychology, or mindfulness and meditation practice.

However, in practice, body and mind exercises are often identified and carried out independently. Their paths may never merge and the result is a disjointed exercise routine that does not support a more relaxed integrated mind and body training system.

Cross Train With Tai Chi

Tai Chi cross training goes a long way to addressing this problem, and is a type of cross training that deepens and integrates the mind-body connection and opens up new neuromuscular pathways (see section 2.5), which in turn not only leads to a greater athletic benefit but also to a more healthy well balanced athlete and persona.

From research undertaken over a number of years, it is well known that if you train your neurological system then your overall performance, whether in sports, business or everyday life will improve.

Tai Chi is the perfect low impact body and mind exercise that can help to counteract the stresses and strains of regular cardiovascular workouts in a way that opens up and strengthens the neuromuscular pathways. This integrated approach to training both the mind and body lead to exercising in a stress-free way, minimising any overuse injury and aiding recovery, particularly when it forms part of a rehabilitation program or plan.

This is just the tip of the iceberg regarding cross training with Tai Chi, as the benefits can be realised by all sportsmen and woman, not just by professional or serious amateur athletes.

Throughout the world today there are millions of people out there who participate in various sports (e.g. Running, Tennis, Badminton, Football, Soccer, Golf, Cricket, Baseball,

1. Introduction

Martial arts, Skiing etc), and do so, not to become the 'best of the best', but to stay fit and healthy.

Also, many athletes:

- Find themselves in a fitness rut, bored with the same old routines and by the same weekday or weekend run!

- Find that their current exercise routine may not be helping them achieve the level of performance improvement they want or expect, and are therefore looking for something a little different to re-motivate them and push them on.

- Take a break from regular exercises or are recovering from injury. They are looking to return or rehabilitate but do not want to replicate their old exercise regime. They are looking for a softer, more internally connected, cross training exercise that replaces one or two of their current scheduled exercise routines. This will then support their recovery from injury and provide a more balanced exercise regime that provides the impetus for further improvement, and re-motivates them to 'get back on track' to achieve their goals.

If you can relate to any of the above, then maybe Tai Chi cross training can fill the void. This allows for the shift away from too many cardiovascular and muscle building exercise

Cross Train With Tai Chi

routines to a form of cross training that integrates the whole body and mind and is the 'Yin' (soft) to your normal 'Yang' (hard) cardiovascular and muscle strengthening exercises.

Cross training with Tai Chi provides a balanced low impact mindful exercise that helps reduce physical and mental stress, reduce anxiety, and stimulate and increase performance levels in everything you do.

So, is Tai Chi for you? You may have reservations, as your training schedule is already at breaking point, or you just don't have the energy to try out yet another new exercise or fad.

To help you decide, ask yourself if any of the following statements apply to you. If they do, then cross training with Tai Chi is recommended.

- You're in good shape but want something more to give you that edge.

- Your fed up doing the same type of exercise and your routine is boring

- You have trouble concentrating and completing mundane tasks

- You are constantly feeling tired and lack energy both at work and in your normal daily life.

1. Introduction

- You've picked up a repetitive strain type of injury as your routine includes completing the same exercise in the same manner time and time again.

- The thought of your exercise schedule creates anxiety and stresses you out

- You're not achieving your sports performance goals

- You want to incorporate a health and wellness element to your routine to strengthen your immune system and make you less prone to injury and illness.

- You want to take your fitness and health to the next level and know more about opening your neuromuscular pathways to achieve even greater performance.

If you're still not convinced, take a look at the many benefits of Tai Chi training.

1.2 Benefits of Cross Training with Tai Chi

As a former semi-professional soccer player and instructor of Tai Chi, I believe cross training with Tai Chi truly fulfils an unmet need in the current market, as it seeks to address the key physical and psychological aspects associated with peak performance and expected results.

Cross Train With Tai Chi

Tai Chi is a well-rounded complete mind and body exercise that can supplement an athlete's training program and lead to improving their performance and overall health and wellness. A number of Tai Chi's benefits are as follows:

- Tai Chi is a low impact stress-free exercise that helps you maintain mind-body balance, both during and after exercise, and keeps you motivated and in good shape.

- Studies have shown that Tai Chi helps to strengthen bone density and the immune system resulting in improved health and overall wellness.

- Tai Chi can prevent overuse injuries and also help athletes to regain leg strength and physical balance after injury.

- If you need to rehabilitate from an injury, such as muscle pulls, strains, or tears, Tai Chi provides the kind of training that allows you to stay in shape and lets your body heal while you exercise.

- Tai Chi provides a level of focused attention and awareness that when combined with practice can lead to enhanced performance.

- Musculoskeletal strength, flexibility, neuromuscular coordination, and reflexes are all improved when practicing Tai Chi.

1. Introduction

- The slow coordinated exercise routines of Tai Chi help to balance out both sides of the body.

- Tai Chi offers many pluses to raise the level of your game. It provides flexibility, balance, strength and modest conditioning of both body and mind.

- All athletes can benefit from applying the principles and ingredients of Tai Chi, including focused intention, effective deep breathing, integrated movement, and moderation.

- The deepened mind-body connection Tai Chi affords can help you see each movement of your chosen sport exactly as you would like it to be.

- Tai Chi abdominal breathing (or belly breathing) can be used as a tool for relaxation; a relaxed athlete is a more efficient, better-coordinated athlete. Relaxation helps to eliminate tension, stress, and anxiety, all of which can impede performance.

- Tai Chi deep breathing helps lower your heart rate, relax your muscles, increase your mind-body connection, and creates a calm, focused state of mind. Especially in high-pressure moments (e.g. penalty kicks in soccer or set or match point in Tennis).

Cross Train With Tai Chi

- Using numerous Tai Chi techniques can help you "get in the zone" while playing any sport.

- Tai Chi can improve your overall health by balancing cardio type training with low impact body and mind training.

- Sports science and sports psychology are starting to understand that you get the greatest athletic benefit from training your neurological system (see section 2.5). Tai Chi uses unfamiliar movement patterns to strengthen your neuromuscular pathways, which in turn helps to improve your coordination, balance, stability, grace and alignment.

- For more serious, and more technical sports specific requirements, Tai Chi offers a strategic approach to exercise where enhanced performance can be obtained by varying your exercise schedule to develop specific skills or mindset.

Hopefully, at this stage, you are intrigued and want to know more about how to cross train with Tai Chi to further enhance your performance, improve your health and re-motivate yourself by doing away with the same old boring routines. The last section of this introduction provides you with an overview of each chapter.

1. Introduction

1.3 What's in the Book?

This book outlines the relevance and use of cross training to increase both physical and mental performance. From understanding the general concept of cross training and how just building stamina or muscle strength is not the only way to cross train, to describing how Tai Chi, and its associated benefits, provide a much more balanced approach to improving performance and overall health and wellness.

I would recommend reading this book in the order it is presented, as it systematically leads the reader on a journey from the basic ideas of cross training to why, and how, Tai Chi is the ideal cross training exercise system. It concludes by recommending two possible training options and discusses how the student can check if their new Tai Chi exercises and practice is resulting in delivering the benefits expected.

A chapter-by-chapter overview is as follows:

Chapter 1 this chapter introduces the reader or student to cross training and the benefits that can be realised by cross training with Tai Chi.

Chapter 2 introduces the background and history of Tai Chi before explaining how this traditional Chinese martial art can contribute to strengthening your life force energy (Qi), where relaxing the mind and body through effective and efficient lower abdominal

Cross Train With Tai Chi

breathing is vital to delivering that extra special performance at that key moment. It concludes by taking a look at how Tai Chi's form and function is closely related to a number of sports, and can support improvement in these sports.

Chapter 3 starts by exploring the current thinking on Sports Science and Sports Psychology and how Tai Chi fits into this area of sports development and improvement. The importance of stress reduction, mindfulness and how Tai Chi can help an athlete achieve a calm mind in a high-pressure situation is explained. This is followed by an introduction to Tai Chi's Ten Essential Principles, and how their understanding and application is fundamental to achieving peak performance and being 'in the zone' more frequently.

Chapter 4 introduces the reader and potential Tai Chi student to a typical program and training schedule, by offering advice on finding a teacher and class, or enrolling on an online Tai Chi course or program. The chapter concludes by outlining the elements of a typical online Tai Chi training course.

Chapter 5 seeks out answers to the question: How Do I Know Tai Chi is working? Student expectations are

1. Introduction

discussed before explaining how students can, and should, track their progress. The chapter concludes with a systematic approach to reviewing a students learning outcomes, supported by the completion of a feedback questionnaire, three to six months after starting a 'Face to Face' class or online Tai Chi course.

A method for reviewing and analysing the results is explained to provide the student with feedback on how far they have come on their Tai Chi Journey. The student is able to obtain pragmatic feedback on whether Tai Chi is working for them, and also reinforce the need for continuous deliberate practice to further improve their Tai Chi, primary sports performance, and overall health and wellness.

Chapter 6 concludes the book by listing various resources (e.g. internet, books, articles) that can be researched to deepen the student's traditional Tai Chi knowledge and skill.

2. Cross Training With Tai Chi

2.1 An Introduction to Tai Chi

Tai Chi's diversity and richness derive from being made up of multiple components, including many physical, cognitive, and psychosocial ingredients.

Tai Chi is a mind-body exercise rooted in multiple Chinese traditions, including Martial Arts, Traditional Chinese Medicine (TCM) and Chinese philosophy. Tai Chi training integrates slow movements with breathing and cognitive skills (for example, mindfulness, visualisation and imagery). It aims to strengthen, relax and integrate the physical body and mind, enhance the natural flow of Qi (more on this in section 2.2), and improve an athlete's performance whilst strengthening their immune system.

What is referred to, as Tai Chi throughout this book is a simplified abbreviation of a more formal name 'Tai Chi Chuan', which is translated as 'Supreme Ultimate Boxing' – straight from its martial arts roots.

17

Cross Train With Tai Chi

Tai Chi has rich intertwined historical origins, including threads linking it to Chinese martial arts, healing arts, philosophy and spiritual practices that span thousands of years. However, it's more recent history, over the past three centuries, has solidified and formalised the art of Tai Chi.

Tai Chi has adapted to changing cultural needs and opportunities in China. It has evolved from a secret, orally transmitted self-defence system in the early 1800s, to a more widely shared fighting art used to train the military, before becoming a publicly shared exercise system for personal development and longevity through the 1900s, and up to the present day.

Tai Chi's expansion and explosion into the West over the last 50 years or so has included a more structured interface with science and evidence-based biomedicine, along with a Westerner's hunger for holistic health and philosophical wisdom from the East.

Its overall history includes the interweaving of three deep influences of Chinese culture. These three influences are martial arts, healing arts, and philosophy. If your interest has been stimulated in these three influential areas, then more detailed information can be found in numerous books and Internet sources referred to in chapter 6.

2. Cross Training with Tai Chi

Yin/Yang Philosophy

At it's very highest level of understanding; opposing Yin and Yang elements are thought to have made the universe and need to be kept in balanced harmony.

Tai Chi derives its name from the concept of Yin and Yang. The symbol of Yin and Yang depicts two complimentary polar opposites that, together, create a dynamic, balanced, integrated, and interdependent whole.

Yin and Yang philosophy, when applied to Tai Chi Chuan, is all about the movements being created from the emergence and changing energies of Yin and Yang.

Yin and Yang are not absolutes, within Yang, there is Yin and vice versa. Both Yin and Yang are opposing and supporting qualities that exist because the other exists. As stated in the Tai Chi classics – first there is Wuji (a state of nothingness, non-being or being in harmony with the universe), and then there is Tai Chi, born out of Wuji. At Wuji there is no Yin/Yang separation, at Tai Chi there is a continuous flow and relationship between Yin and Yang energies.

Most people understand the basic Yin (i.e. night, soft, slow, black, dark, cold) and Yang (i.e. day, hard, fast, white, light, hot) elements when considered in everyday life. However, it's important that these are understood in the context of learning Tai Chi to further develop your Tai Chi skills once the basic movements are learnt.

Cross Train With Tai Chi

Everything in Tai chi can be connected to Yin and Yang. The idea of Yin and Yang can seem abstract, but in Tai Chi, the concept is used in a very practical way. It means that we are comparing opposite things. A classic example of Yin and Yang is to imagine the sun shining on the side of a hill. One side of the hill will be in the shadow and the other side of the hill will be in the light. In Yin/Yang theory, the shadow side is Yin and the bright side is Yang.

Another example can be made with sports cross training. If we take a look at the Yin and Yang elements of what is generally deemed normal cross training, we can see that the cardiovascular and muscle strengthening exercises are considered to be Yang in nature and the more mindful or meditative exercises are characterised as Yin. The issue here is a question of balance – as the primary sport is normally Yang focused and the cross training cardio activity tends to be Yang driven. This is unbalanced, as there are limited, or no, Yin related exercises or activity. Cross training with Tai Chi seeks to help bridge the gap and address this Yin/Yang balance, thereby providing the athlete with a moderated fully integrated mind and body Yin workout, which in turn helps to strengthen the athletes' immune system making them less prone to illness and injury.

Tai Chi practice is full of opposites that can be seen through the lens of Yin and Yang. For instance: postures

2. Cross Training with Tai Chi

have movements that go up (Yang) or go down (Yin). Many Tai Chi postures and movements also go forward and backward, right and left, or open and close. All of these can be seen as different expressions of Yin and Yang.

The idea of Yin and Yang can also be applied to different kinds of Tai Chi practice. Sometimes we train in a Yin way, for example, when we practice holding a single posture. Practice that is a little more still, passive or quiet, can be considered more Yin. Moving practice is more Yang. Quiet practice is often referred to as "quiescent" practice.

Generally, we consider Yin movements to be soft, neutralising, and empty, while Yang movements are hard, energy delivering, and full. For each technique or movement there is a Yin phase, which is focused on storing energy, and then a Yang phase, which is focused on the delivery of the stored energy. In movement, the idea of Yin and Yang can also be applied to weight distribution in the legs, which is sometimes referred to as "empty" and "full." Step by step, we first learn to recognise the Yin/Yang relationship within ourselves throughout the forms, postures, and sequences.

Examples of the general concepts of Yin and Yang in the techniques of Tai Chi are as follows:

Cross Train With Tai Chi

Yin	*Yang*
Back of the body	Front of the body
Lower body	Upper body
Palm facing body	Palm facing away from body
Leg that is empty	Leg that supports the weight
Soft movement	Hard Movement
Defending	Attacking

Tai Chi training embodies this Yin/Yang concept at multiple levels. The most obvious are the physical level, as Tai Chi is an exercise that aims to strengthen, stretch, balance, coordinate and integrate the left and right halves of the body, the upper and lower parts of the body, and the extremities of the body, with the inside or core.

At a more subtle level, Tai Chi integrates body and mind. Body movements are coordinated with rhythmic, conscious breathing and multiple cognitive and emotional components. These include focused attention and mindfulness, feeling awareness, increased sensitivity, visualisation, and intention.

2. Cross Training with Tai Chi

At a higher level, Tai Chi sensitises and integrates with your social and physical environment. At an interpersonal level, being in tune with other people, particularly those that you may be in competition with, helps you to learn to read, and appropriately respond, to their movement and body language.

This internal/external integration is one of Tai Chi's many secrets as a martial art. By becoming extremely sensitive to your opponents energy and movement, you learn to neutralise, deflect and follow their attack to disarm or defeat them. The same could be said for many individual and team sports.

For example, when distance running you are able to respond to another athletes sudden injection of pace at just the right time to hopefully stay connected and in touch with them. The same could be said for team sports, where individual battles are going on all over the field of play, where you can feel a change in the game, or the opponents surge, of lack of energy, and can positively respond, as appropriate.

2.2 What is Qi?

Qi (or Chi – pronounced Chee) is the circulating life force energy whose existence and properties are the basis of Chinese philosophy and medicine.

Cross Train With Tai Chi

You don't need to subscribe to, or learn about, Tai Chi's roots in Chinese philosophy and medicine to realise the many benefits of cross training with Tai Chi. However, the concepts of Qi can illuminate your learning and practice.

Qi (Chi)

Traditional Chinese Medicine (TCM) states or believes that Qi can be regulated by applying alternative therapies such as Acupuncture, Tuina (Chinese massage), Herbs, Qi Gong (Energy work) and Tai Chi.

Tai Chi helps to unblock, strengthen and encourage the smooth flow of Qi throughout the body. The ancient Chinese described it as "life force energy", as they believed Qi permeates everything and linked their surroundings together. They likened it to the flow of energy around and through the body, forming a cohesive and functioning unit. By understanding the Qi's rhythm and flow they believed they could guide exercises and treatments to prevent illness, provide stability and longevity, leading to improved health and overall wellness.

Traditional Chinese Medicine (TCM) asserts that the body has natural patterns of Qi that circulate in channels called meridians. In TCM, symptoms of various illnesses are believed to be the product of disrupted, stagnated, blocked, or unbalanced Qi throughout the body's meridians, as well as deficiencies or imbalances of Qi in the organs. TCM seeks to

2. Cross Training with Tai Chi

relieve these imbalances by adjusting the circulation of Qi using a variety of techniques including herbs, food therapy, Acupuncture, Tuina (massage) and physical training regimens, such as Qigong, Tai Chi, and other internal martial arts training.

If we take Acupuncture as an example, many people have considered or received Acupuncture treatment to relieve their health related issues. Acupuncture involves the insertion of needles into superficial structures of the body (skin, subcutaneous tissue, muscles) at acupuncture points to rebalance and strengthen the flow of Qi.

If you wish to deepen your understanding and knowledge of Qi and TCM, I recommend reading Ted J Kaptchuk's excellent book 'Chinese Medicine: The Web That Has No Weaver.'

2.3 Mind/Body Integration

As we have seen, Tai Chi is an exercise that integrates both body and mind and this, in turn, contributes to improving personal performance and overall health and wellness.

How does Tai Chi achieve this?

There are a number of active ingredients, that when combined, result in a full mind/body workout. Awareness

Cross Train With Tai Chi

and Postural Alignment coupled with the 'Ten Essential Principles' of Yang family Tai Chi (see section 3.4), provide the foundations for understanding and practicing Tai Chi as a fully active mind/body exercise.

Self-Awareness (Mindfulness and Attention)

This ingredient relates to becoming more aware of, and at greater ease with, what is happening within the body and mind at any given moment. Awareness of moment-to-moment sensations allows you to train and hold your attention or mental focus, providing you with a tool to manage distracting thoughts and mental chatter. As a result, you are more engaged with the physical tasks at hand and much more in the moment.

This heightened self-awareness leads to sustained focused attention without over thinking. Through slow, deliberate movements and attention to breath and mental quality, Tai Chi fosters acute self-awareness. This includes bodily sensation, thoughts and emotions, and the overall connection between mind and body.

Becoming bodily aware allows you to sense your inner body and identify areas of tension or strain, as well as movements that feel graceful or clumsy. This awareness can play a significant part in your rehabilitation from injury, or in improving your primary sports performance.

2. Cross Training with Tai Chi

Tai Chi can help you to enhance your focus, awareness, and sensitivity so that you can clearly and effectively respond to any situation; such as taking a penalty in a soccer match, serving for the set or match in Tennis, or simply walking on an uneven path or lifting an object.

Having addressed bodily awareness, let us not forget mental focus. Tai Chi's emphasis on moment-to-moment bodily awareness also trains our mental focus.

In today's very busy, multi-tasking technological society we rarely take time to slow down, to notice and concentrate fully on what's happening in the present moment. Our ability to stay focused on tasks in the present moment has greatly reduced. However, during Tai Chi practice you are continuously required to notice what is happening at any given moment, paying attention to the quality of movement, posture, breath, balance and the impact of the environment around you, including the people around you.

Tai Chi provides the type of cross training for athletes that will help them to improve their focused attention and mindfulness while reducing their everyday 'monkey mind' chatter, allowing them to concentrate on doing their best at any given moment.

'Hold on a minute', I can hear some of you saying, 'I already practice mindfulness and meditation to improve my ability to stay in the present moment'.

Cross Train With Tai Chi

I agree, that while practicing mindfulness and meditation also provides the foundation and skills to remain in the present moment, neither of them, when practiced on their own, fully unify or integrate the body and mind elements like Tai Chi.

Tai Chi provides an exercise or cross training workout that expertly tunes the body and mind to deliver effective and efficient mindful movement as one whole.

Let's take a look in a little more detail at awareness from a feeling perspective. In the book 'Zen Body Being: An Enlightened Approach to Physical Skill, Grace and Power,' Peter Ralston explains how developing 'Feeling Awareness' is very important for anyone interested in body improvement and skill enhancement. I have included a couple of Peter Ralston's exercises below as they are particularly beneficial to athletes and the Tai Chi student.

Exercise 1

We often take for granted our body awareness and feelings even though feeling is what movement is all about, and it is also how movement is perceived. To experience this spend some time doing the following.

Lift your hand a few times while investigating these two questions:

2. Cross Training with Tai Chi

- How do you 'will' your hand to go up?

- What actually gets the hand up?

You will find that in order to lift your hand, you generate a feeling. It's not necessarily easy to break it down since the feeling you generate is the one you call 'lifting your hand'.

How do you know your hand is up once you have lifted it? Try closing your eyes and raise your hand. Given that your eyes are closed, notice how it is 'you' that manages to lift the hand, and how it is 'you' that knows its moving, and how 'you' know it's in the air once lifted. Excluding sight, you perceive where the arm is by feeling the arm is raised up. You know because you can feel it.

Take a few moments to study this until you can experience for yourself the subtle sensation, the feeling-impulse that is actually responsible for lifting your hand. Also, isolate the sensations that allow you to perceive where your arm is in space. Notice that without this sensory feedback you would have no idea where your arm is.

These feelings are usually taken for granted and so we lose touch with them. With practice we can make these distinctions again. As a result, we will develop much greater control and mastery of both our actions and awareness.

Cross Train With Tai Chi

Exercise 2

In this exercise, we are now seeking to increase our sensitivity to feeling-awareness on many levels, and to become very sensitive to feeling the whole body.

Put your attention on your whole body all at once. When you put your attention on your body, what is there, what do you feel? Do you feel the whole body, every part?

Now, take a few moments and starting with your toes, try to consciously feel every cubic inch of your body, all the way to the top of your head. Unless you have done this a lot you will probably miss a great deal, and some of what you miss you may not notice because you cannot feel it. Repeated practice, however, will bring increased awareness. As you do it again, even for a short time, you should be able to feel your body a little more each time you repeat the exercise.

How did you feel? Did you notice an increased feeling awareness? Imagine the benefits that can be realised if your self-awareness is developed so that you heighten the sensitivity of your body, and can make minuscule adjustments to your movement to improve your sporting technique.

Both exercises bring us back to feeling awareness basics. They call for us to identify what it feels like to experience feeling awareness when undertaking simple movements or just standing. We now need to take a look at the second ingredient, Postural integration and alignment.

2. Cross Training with Tai Chi

Postural Integration and Alignment

This ingredient is closely associated with a number of the essential principles of Tai Chi as it relates to body posture and alignment. Building on the essential principles such as 'Lift up your head as if suspended from above', 'shoulders down and relaxed', 'chest soft' and upper back rounded', 'lower back lengthening', tail bone under' (see section 3.4 for more details), Tai Chi trains you to maximise your body's physical potential and to find alignments that afford safe, unstrained, and graceful postures and movement.

This focus on postural alignment can help you undertake movements in your primary sport with less energy, and can contribute to you being stronger late in the game or in the race.

With feeling awareness and good postural alignment, you realise that you can feel the movement of the arms, hands and fingers, right down to your feet and toes. Or, you can feel how your breathing affects your composure and anxiety, and aligns and connects your ribs and spine. You are now on your way to discovering full body integration and unity, where and any one part of the body affects all others.

The same can be said of Tai Chi movement, where any one part of the body affects all others. The same can also be said, but not often realised or understood for most sports. It's just that this method or approach to other sports is rarely considered or explored.

Cross Train With Tai Chi

This structural integration and alignment enhances your primary sports potential, as aligning and moving your body in a Tai Chi manner can lead to higher levels of performance. Also, there is a real chance that you will be less prone to injuries, or they will be less frequent, resulting in a reduction in the time it takes to recuperate from injury.

Tai Chi's effective postural integration can also lead to more efficient movement patterns and decreased levels of muscle contraction or co-activation, which in turn leads to decreased muscular and joint stress.

By its very nature, Tai Chi emphasises slow, coordinated and integrated movements. Changes from one movement to another unfold and reflect functional movement principles related to human biomechanics. In addition to postural integration and alignment and the creation of new neuromuscular pathways (see section 2.5), the slow movements give you the time to sense your body's position, make appropriate modifications, and organise the various parts of your body so they all work together.

The concept of postural or structural integration is related to the evolutionary biological principle of form and function, where shapes and patterns of movement have functional consequences across many body systems. For example, if you improve your structural organisation, you will likely improve your physiological function. If your chest and ribs

2. Cross Training with Tai Chi

collapse less you are able to breath more efficiently. Just think how beneficial this is for someone who may be an endurance athlete!

2.4 Tai Chi Relaxation and Breathing

Relaxation

Relaxation in Tai Chi is not easily defined and often means different things to different people. For example, to some relaxing is to rest, especially after a workout or work. To others, relaxation means slouching on the sofa in front of the television.

However, in Tai Chi, relaxation takes this one step further as it's a much more dynamic. Tai Chi was developed as an internal martial art, a soft or relaxed martial art where you need to be dynamically relaxed to yield to your opponents attack, using their strength and force to redirect their attack in readiness for your own counter attack.

In Tai Chi the whole body needs to be relaxed, but this idea of relaxation is not limpness, dropping your guard or kicking back on the couch. Tai Chi's relaxation principle is based on a more active or dynamic form of relaxation, where relaxation is a qualitative mind-body state, which the Chinese refer to as being 'Sung.'

Cross Train With Tai Chi

Sung is often defined as the limbs and body feeling extended and expanded, and is developed by loosening and opening the joints to aid the natural flow of Qi. Section 3.4 outlines a number of essential postural principles (shoulders relaxed, elbows down, chest soft, waist relaxed, hips loose etc), which when applied correctly supports the development of Sung.

When practicing Tai Chi you use gentle movements and effective and efficient breathing to help remove or reduce physical and emotional tensions, freeing up the underlying functional structures and aiding the development and flow of Qi, which, when combined with loosening and opening of the joints, contributes to the development of Sung, or dynamic relaxation in Tai Chi. This, in turn, results in your body becoming energised, while in a relaxed and active state.

Just imagine how your performance in other sports could be improved if you are able to enter a dynamically relaxed state when required, to focus the mind, reduce the tension in the body and perfectly execute a technique, thus setting you up to make that final push to win the race or improve your personal best. This can be enhanced even further when effective and efficient breathing is also activated.

Effective Breathing

Effective efficient mindful breathing is another key ingredient. Tai Chi's lower abdominal breathing can affect

34

2. Cross Training with Tai Chi

health, wellbeing and personal development. Deeper abdominal breathing fully utilises the lung capacity and aids speedy recovery (i.e. reduces your heart rate), helps calm the mind and regulates emotions. It also serves to improve awareness, intention and structural awareness.

Breath awareness and relevant breath training exercises play an important role in Tai Chi and all Eastern healing traditions. Breath awareness and training has also been integrated into biomedical stress reduction programs and sports training, and Tai Chi is ideally placed to be integrated into these type of programs.

Tai Chi breath training, when combined with postural alignment and dynamic relaxation, provides a more flexible and balanced structure so that your body can inhale and exhale with less effort. In simple terms this means the volume of air inhaled in a relaxed, upright and open Tai Chi posture is much greater than the volume you can inhale in a slouched, tense posture, typical of today's stressed out athlete or desk worker.

From a health perspective, Tai Chi's greater breathing awareness and efficiency are associated with a reduced risk of heart disease, and a positive effect on your nervous system, which in turn can further improve the capacity and efficiency of your breathing.

It is well known that during times of emotional stress our nervous system is stimulated, resulting in numerous

Cross Train With Tai Chi

physiological changes, including a faster heart rate and rapid shallow breathing. Incorporating Tai Chi and effective breathing exercises in your cross training program or exercise schedule can help to minimise the impact of stress and anxiety at those key times in a match or game, enabling you to perform more naturally and as expected.

For example, on average you breathe in excess of 20,000 times per day, so it naturally follows that efficient, mindful breathing patterns have the potential to significantly enhance and sustain your health, which in turn may result in you living a longer life. It may also provide you with that additional burst of energy to turn potential failure into success, no matter what activity or task you are undertaking.

As you can see, the integrated mind (awareness, intention and breathing) and body (relaxation and postural alignment) ingredients of cross training with Tai Chi provide a unified whole body exercise, that would complement any athlete's primary sport and support their further development and improvement, while enhancing their health and overall well-being.

2.5 Opening Neuromuscular Pathways

Most of the current trend of cross training exercise focuses on further development of stamina and strength, whereas Tai Chi enhances flexibility, balance, strength, and goes some

2. Cross Training with Tai Chi

way to helping the athlete enhance their focus and reflexes while improving their range of movement, thereby opening up new neuromuscular pathways. This makes Tai Chi an excellent exercise if you are rehabilitating from a sports injury, as it helps to keep you in shape and lets your body heal while you recover.

The opening of new neuromuscular pathways (or Brain-muscle connection) while cross training with Tai Chi or carrying out basic Tai Chi exercise drills is very important and beneficial.

The neuromuscular junction is the point at which an electrical impulse from the nervous system (your brain) is passed to the muscle. These impulses signal the muscle fibres to fire and produce movement. Most of our daily movement is so familiar that these pathways are 'well worn'. But when we learn a new movement, these pathways can be somewhat 'fuzzy'.

For example, when learning to ride a bicycle a child is unfamiliar with the movement; they are trying to coordinate their balance (core stability), with the motion of their legs on the pedals. The movement feels new and difficult because the brain-muscle connection has never been used in that way.

However, as the child practices these movements and they're neuromuscular connections become more efficient

Cross Train With Tai Chi

the child begins to acquire the balance and coordination necessary for riding a bicycle. The child adapts neurologically to perform the new skill.

The same is true of most sports. They require similar balance and coordination and when the motion is repeated in practice our body adapts neurologically and physically.

Tai Chi 'body work' drills and 'form' practice take specific movements or complimentary movements, isolate them and 'slow' them down so that they can be practiced at slower speeds. The slow low impact movements of Tai Chi allow the athlete to focus specifically on a particular movement and perform it with full awareness and mind-body coordination. For example, when running the weaknesses and imbalances of our body affect our body structure and gait. Basically, when running fatigued everything begins to break down, and as your postural alignment starts to falter you become less efficient, which in turn impacts your performance.

The repetition of Tai Chi slow low impact exercise and drills 'beats down' the path of the brain-muscle connection so that execution of the movement becomes more connected, effective and more efficient. These "newly trained" connections can aid a fatigued athlete so that they can maintain postural alignment and awareness and perform as expected, even when tired.

38

2. Cross Training with Tai Chi

2.6 Tai Chi for Sports

"Extraordinary performances come out of a process of continuous, regular and physical and mental practice. The mindset of an extraordinary athlete is relaxed but focused and open to even higher achievements. Real success or victory is measured by the quality of that very process of attention and mindful involvement, practice, and commitment".

Chungliang Al Huang and Jerry Lynch,
Thinking Body, Dancing Mind

We are already aware that many athletes cross train to improve their primary sports performance. They generally participate in a number of exercise activities in addition to their chosen, or primary sport. They do this to help prevent over-use injuries, relieve the monotony of repeating the same training program, and you can often choose the best qualities of other sports to enhance your physical and mental skills.

This section outlines how you can integrate the principles and mind-body focus and awareness of Tai Chi to perform better in your chosen sport. Basically, this is where strength, stamina, coordination, speed, flexibility, balance, and resistance to injury are all key.

Tai Chi provides the kind of exercise that can improve all these elements as they relate to all sports, whether it's the

Cross Train With Tai Chi

accuracy of your tennis serve, the smooth flow of your golf swing or the carving of your ski turns. Tai Chi training also helps to balance out both sides of the body, enabling the athlete to be always ready to go left or right, rather than be stuck in an unbalanced position.

And, more importantly, Tai Chi's 70 percent rule prevents overtraining and injury. The 70 percent rule requires the athlete to train at 70% of their full 100% intensity. By exercising with moderation it helps the athlete to identify their limits. If you know your limits the risk of burn out or further injury can be minimised.

Athletes can benefit from applying the principles and ingredients of Tai Chi, including intention, effective breathing, integrated body movement and moderation.

Athletes often use visualisation and imagery to enhance their performance. When you cross train with Tai Chi you will also use visualisation to train the mind, as you would muscle; and musculoskeletal strength, flexibility and neuromuscular coordination and reflexes are all improved.

We have now come a long way in explaining how Tai Chi should be considered as a cross training exercise to develop greater expertise and improve your primary sports performance.

The list below shows the people and specific sports that can benefit from cross training with Tai Chi.

2. Cross Training with Tai Chi

- All sportsmen and women.

- Professional and amateur athletes in a wide range of sports (i.e. Athletics, Baseball, Basketball, Martial Arts, Tennis, Golf, Football, Soccer, Rugby, Cricket, Running, Walking, Triathlon, Swimming, Cycling etc).

- People in the media, especially celebrities and entertainers

- Athletes who would benefit from 'one on one' programs to give them that extra edge, leading to even greater levels of improvement.

- Anyone wanting to improve their overall health and mental wellness, especially those suffering from depression, or recovering from a degenerative or rehabilitating illness or disease.

- Athletes recovering from injury and need a low impact exercise to support them on their way to full recovery.

There have been a number of athletes in competitive sports that have discovered the benefits of Tai Chi. Former NBA Boston Celtics star Robert Parish credited Tai Chi for his durability. Skier Ted Ligety was a dedicated and focused Tai Chi student among the members of the US Men's Alpine

Cross Train With Tai Chi

Ski team in 2005 and had a breakout season. In February 2006, he won a gold medal at the Winter Olympic Games in Turin, Italy.

Tai Chi is an excellent sports training exercise because its goal is to cultivate balance, calmness, and full body integration while performing with less effort. During Tai Chi practice you learn about the importance of the waist, as Tai Chi practitioners are taught to start the movement from the centre or waist. The waist can be thought of as a wide belt, of approximately four inches (10cm), all the way around the body. This is why many Tai Chi masters and instructors talk about the waist being part of the lower back as this waist movement integrates the movement with the spine.

This is especially helpful for Skateboarding, Snowboarding, Surfing and Skiing. Likewise, in Baseball, Golf, Tennis and Racquetball you swing from the centre, or waist, to hit the ball.

Let's take a look at how Tai Chi supports, and can help improve performance, or reduce injury, in a number of sports.

Tai Chi for Tennis

In Waysun Liao's book, 'The Essence of Tai Chi,' the Tai Chi Classics state that all movement is started, or rooted in the feet, controlled or steered by the waist, and expressed by the hands. A tennis player knows that all good ground

2. Cross Training with Tai Chi

strokes (forehand and backhand) use very similar movements, as you move your feet into position, turn your waist to begin the shot, and hit the ball with the racquet and follow through with the arm and hand.

Tai Chi can help the tennis player:

- Become more balanced both physically, mentally and emotionally.

- Obtain a higher degree of balance as the weight is shifted from side to side chasing down an opponents shot while preparing for the next shot.

- Coordinate and connect the whole body when serving, so as to integrate the turning and weight transfer to allow for a more relaxed and powerful serve.

- Apply the same mind and body coordination when playing ground strokes or volleying.

- Recover from a hard fought match or injury.

The balanced stepping and weight transfer movements of Tai Chi translate directly to the tennis court. Also, when your mind and body act as one integrated whole you become emotionally centred and focus more on the actual game your playing.

Cross Train With Tai Chi

In W. Timothy Gallwey's classic book, *The Inner Game of Tennis*, he served up a unique way of looking at Tennis. As the book's title suggests, it's focused on the 'inner game,' and what goes on in a tennis players mind and how to apply this to the outer physical game on a tennis court.

Much of Gallwey's thinking is very similar to the Tai Chi concept of 'getting out of your own way' to let your best game emerge. His theories are based on concentration (i.e. mindfulness) and self-awareness, where the most important first step is to see and feel what you are doing to increase your awareness of what's actually happening on court. This is very similar to Tai Chi developing feeling awareness, sensitivity and improving postural integration and alignment.

Tai Chi for Golf

Tai Chi Body movement and a Golf swing are very similar. A combination of relaxation, effective breathing and all parts of the body (upper, middle and lower) working together equates to a more balanced efficient swing.

Tai Chi and the golf swing share some basic principles.

- First, you relax into the stance and feel rooted into the earth.

- Second, you deepen your breath, as this lowers your heart rate (which is extremely important when

2. Cross Training with Tai Chi

participating in Golf tournaments where your nerves can easily get the better of you, especially on the first tee) and helps relax the muscles and increase the mind-body connection, thereby creating a calm, focused state to set up your golf swing.

- Third, you shift your weight, turn your waist and coil your body around a vertical axis to build up the power.

- Fourth, you uncoil your body to release the full power when making contact with the ball. The power results from the integrated connection of the lower body (feet and Legs), middle body (waist and hips) and Upper body (torso, arms, and hands). The golfer is then rooted in the feet, with the power developed in the legs, controlled by the waist, and extended out by the arms and hands and executed with the clubface. Throughout the swing movement, the golf club is effectively an extension of the arm and the whole body is integrated to achieve the power of shot required.

Tai Chi helps to build lower body leg strength and flexibility thereby improving a golfers balance when starting, transitioning and completing the swing. This, in turn, provides the golfer with a more fluid relaxed swing, better tempo and more distance on their shots.

Cross Train With Tai Chi

The concept of swinging from the waist may also help reduce "golfer's back," a repetitive strain type of injury to the lower back. By creating the swing from a relaxed area or band below the navel the twisting of the torso is lessened. This relaxed motion allows the entire force of the waist turning to be projected outward through the hands and club into the ball. Many golfers discover that they can drive the ball much farther after practicing Tai Chi for only a few months.

A student of Tai Chi recognises the importance of excellent form and function. Physical technique and a calm mental focus are fundamental to proper form, or the ideal fully integrated and unified mind-body golf swing.

The practicing Tai Chi student develops technique, focus, and awareness in slow motion. This slow motion movement in Tai Chi demands a high degree of self-awareness, practice, and persistence, as faults become readily apparent. To achieve proper form, the Tai Chi student calls upon the use of the mind and the body in a methodically balanced way. This is often way beyond where most golfers or athletes go to improve their performance.

In Tai Chi, technique must be clearly executed. The student strives to execute even the smallest technique exactly. As we practice the movements we continuously work to connect, or string together, all the parts of the body (upper,

2. Cross Training with Tai Chi

middle, lower) as we increase our focused intention to improve our skill level and control.

Tai Chi enables the student to reach a point where they have physically and mentally internalised the movements of the Tai Chi form, and through repetition improve the quality of their practice, thus deepening their Tai Chi skills. In golf, there are similar actions that take place during the act of striking the ball with accuracy and power.

The haphazard uninformed golf player may occasionally hit a decent shot but he cannot hope to compete with the golfer whose effective relaxed swing leads to delivering an accurate and powerful shot. The golfer with an effective and efficient swing, like the Tai Chi player, is the player who through countless hours of practice masters movements that result in repeating them again and again.

As any golfer who is determined to reduce their handicap to five or below, will tell you, 'It's impossible to play great golf without an excellent swing that is repeatable.' The repeating accurate and powerful swing is mastered through the correct repetition of fundamentals in form to produce quality shots under all kinds of pressure and conditions.

In summary, and as with Tai Chi, effective golf form requires specific moves to be carried out in a balanced, relaxed and focused manner. The essentials of Tai Chi are very similar to the essentials of golf. Through practice and

Cross Train With Tai Chi

application of the Ten Essential Principles of Tai Chi (see section 3.4) the golfer has the potential to lower their handicap. An investigation and inclusion of the Ten Essential Principles of Tai Chi reveal fundamentals that, if practiced purposefully and conscientiously, should lead to an effective and reliable accurate golf swing.

Tai Chi for Soccer and Basketball

Of course, the mental acuity, balance, and self-esteem Tai Chi encourages are also beneficial for other types of sports, such as Soccer and Basketball. It is well known that Phil Jackson (L.A. Lakers basketball team coach) introduced Tai Chi as part of their training.

As outlined in both Tennis and Golf the integrated relaxed Tai Chi principles are paramount to moving more fluidly and to bring about the kind of focused self-awareness and calmness that would also benefit the Soccer or Basketball player.

Let's take a more in-depth look at Soccer. In the English Premier League, and many of the other high-profile European leagues, the pressure to perform is at an all time high. The ever increasing social and general media focus, and the high expectations of the soccer club, from both senior management and the fans, results in increased player stress and anxiety, leading to problems maintaining performance

2. Cross Training with Tai Chi

and focus, both on and off the field. This, in turn, can contribute to an individual losing self-belief and confidence in their ability while potentially increasing mental health issues, such as depression.

Let's take a look at soccer from a physical perspective. For example, it's late in the game and completing normal physical moves are getting tougher and tougher, your physical ability has started to falter, and you have reached the meltdown threshold. This is where it gets more difficult to execute the next pass or run the length of the field to make that last gasp tackle to prevent an opponent from scoring. It's not just energetic fatigue, it's your coordination, balance, stability, grace, alignment; it's all of these rolled up in one.

As outlined previously, it is well known that you get the greatest athletic benefit from training your neurological system. Tai Chi uses unfamiliar movement patterns to strengthen your neurological system and your coordination, range of movement, awareness, focus, reflexes, balance, stability, grace and alignment. The opening up of new neuromuscular pathways enables the soccer player to operate in a more dynamically relaxed manner throughout the match. This, in turn, makes it far less likely that they will reach the meltdown threshold and can still excel right through to the final whistle.

Cross-training with Tai Chi can also help to prevent overuse injuries. If you need to rehabilitate from a soccer

Cross Train With Tai Chi

injury, such as muscle pulls, strains, or tears, Tai Chi exercise allows you to stay in shape and lets your body heal while you recover.

If we now take a look at the mental side of a soccer game, we already know that extraordinary performances come out of a process of continuous, regular physical and mental practice. The mindset of an excellent soccer player is relaxed but focused and open to ever-higher achievements. Tai Chi provides a level of attention and mindful involvement, commitment, and practice to enhance a soccer player's performance. Soccer players can benefit from applying many of the ingredients and principles of Tai Chi, including intention, deep breathing, integrated movement, and moderation.

The deepened mind-body connection Tai Chi affords can help you see each soccer movement, pass or shot, exactly as you would like it to be. Tai Chi breathing can be used as a tool for relaxation; a relaxed soccer or basketball player is a more efficient, better-coordinated player. Relaxation can help to minimise tension, stress, and anxiety, all of which impede individual performance and overall team performance. Effective deep (or belly) breathing helps lower your heart rate, relax your muscles, increase your mind-body connection, raise confidence levels, and create a calm, focused state of mind. This is especially useful in high-

2. Cross Training with Tai Chi

pressure situations or moments. For example when taking a penalty kick in soccer, or a free throw in basketball.

Tai Chi for Baseball

The benefits of cross training Tai Chi for Baseball are very similar to Golf and Tennis. A number of positions, including the batter, pitcher and fielders can all benefit. Let's take a look at some examples:

- Tai Chi's ability to improve balance is excellent for infielders, as they move and reach quickly and sharply.

- Just before a Baseball pitcher throws a pitch, they must hold and balance on one leg for a moment or so. This point of balance can help create the force and accuracy of the pitch. Tai Chi exercises provide the natural platform for improving leg strength and stability.

- An effective Baseball swing requires a strong foundation, with a feeling in the feet as if rooted into the earth. In Tai Chi, this rootedness is paramount to smooth integrated movement. Once rooted the batter set's the bat and swings from the waist/relaxed centre. This relaxed movement is fundamental to integrating the upper and lower body movement and is an essential ingredient to developing your Baseball and

Cross Train With Tai Chi

Tai Chi skills. With the energy rooted in the feet, developed by the legs, controlled by the waist and transitioned through the back to the arms and bat gives the Baseball player an effective, relaxed and powerful baseball swing.

- As for Tennis, Golf and Soccer above, the same relaxed focused mind-body benefits can be realised.

Tai Chi and Endurance Sports (Swimming, Running, Cycling)

Some runners or triathletes exercise with Tai Chi as both a warm-up exercise for their normal workouts, or as an "off day" exercise that is soothing to their joints, yet still keeps their mind and body focused.

Let us take a look at an example, similar to that used in soccer above. It's late in the run, swim or cycle, and it's getting real tough to stay competitive. This is where it gets more difficult to execute the next step to stay with a runner in front of you, it's not just energetic fatigue, it's your proprioception is failing!!

What is Proprioception?

As athletes and humans, we take for granted our body position, motion, and acceleration, as well as the amount of

52

2. Cross Training with Tai Chi

effort being exerted by our muscles. This sense of posture in three-dimensional space is known as proprioception. It's a process that tells us where we are in space, where our structure is in relation to the rest of our body and where and how our body is moving. Therefore, proprioception is your body's feedback system. It's your coordination, balance, stability, grace and alignment. It's all of these rolled up in one.

Your body has millions of receptors (called proprioceptors) embedded in your muscles, connective tissues and joints that are all wired into your nervous system. These receptors constantly inform your central nervous system (CNS) about the status of your joints and muscles, their specific location in space, their degree of flexion and extension, their tension and level of stress.

When your proprioception is failing we often resort to adopting a 'Mind over Matter' approach, where the athlete forces their body to move with sheer mental will. This is often invoked when things start to look and feel bad. When the fears and pain prevail and you begin to question your capability, capacity and sanity. When this happens it takes mental tenacity to keep moving forward. However, 'mind over matter' alone will not put the 'wheels back on your wagon.' Sheer 'mental will' cannot bring back the perfect coordination, alignment, and grace of your swimming stroke or running stride – you need to strengthen your proprioception.

Cross Train With Tai Chi

Miraculously, when running, for example, your central nervous system can make sense of this constant barrage of 'electrical data' and respond to keep your body upright and moving forward. Your logical brain, the one that thinks in words, is incapable of doing this.

Ultimately this is your alliance with gravity. You use the pull of gravity to move your body forward or gravity will pull you to the ground. When you strengthen your alliance with gravity, you will go faster and farther with less energy. It's all about applying good postural alignment while running or competing and training in other endurance related sports. If you execute effective and efficient swimming strokes or running strides well before the 'wheels fall off', you will have some chance of sustaining or even improving your position in the race using less effort and energy. By including Tai Chi in your weekly exercise schedule it will help to strengthen your neurological system and proprioception while balancing the energy in the body to achieve the results required or expected.

And remember, as with all sports, as you train your body to be ready for the next important event or race, you also need to train your mind by incorporating effective breathing into your routine. This will help to quieten and calm the mind and improve your laser-like focused intention. This type of mind-body connected mindfulness can be trained and developed through the regular practice of Tai Chi.

2. Cross Training with Tai Chi

In summary, Tai Chi and its underlying principles and focus can help enhance an athlete's performance, reduce the likelihood of injury and help to recuperate and rehabilitate them from injury.

Examples of how cross training with Tai Chi can enhance the performance of athletes whose primary sport is Tennis, Golf, Soccer, Baseball or an Endurance sport (i.e. Swimming, Running, Cycling etc) has shown that this type of cross training should be considered, as it's an excellent low-impact exercise that helps to create new neuromuscular pathways and strengthen your proprioception. As you are probably aware, you can't change your genetics to be a better athlete, but you can improve your proprioception and mindfulness to become a better athlete.

The sports outlined above were selected to provide examples of how cross training with Tai Chi could be extremely beneficial if you are seeking to improve your performance. What has not been formerly included are the many health and wellness benefits. Practicing Tai Chi helps to strengthen the immune system, making an athlete less prone to illness and injury. It also helps to reduce sports stress and anxiety issues.

Athletes participating in a wide range of sports could also benefit from cross training with Tai Chi. For example:

Cross Train With Tai Chi

- Racket sports (Tennis, Badminton, Squash etc)

- Bat and Ball games (Golf, Baseball, Softball, Cricket, Hockey etc)

- Athletics (Running, Long jump, High jump, Javelin, Discus, Shot Putt, Hammer etc)

- Ball games (Soccer, American Football, Basketball, Handball, Rugby, Aussie rules football etc)

- Water Sports (Swimming, Skiing, Water Polo, etc)

- Martial Arts (Kung Fu, Karate, Taekwondo, etc)

- Winter sports (Skiing, Snowboarding, Bob-sleighing, etc)

2.7 Why do we need to balance our Energy?

As we have seen in sections 2.1 and 2.2, understanding and the adoption of Yin/Yang energetic balance in everything we do in sports and our daily life is paramount to improving performance, health and overall wellbeing.

In typical Yang, high intensive, cardiovascular sports, the body and mind are trained one way, and even if the normal muscular or cardiovascular cross training is added to an

2. Cross Training with Tai Chi

athlete's training program it still tends to be focused on stamina and strength training, which is Yang in nature. Where is that Yin/Yang balance?

The Yin part of training is therefore missing. Sometimes meditation or mindfulness is added to an athlete's training regime, and while this is better than nothing it still does not do enough to balance the strong Yang energy with the softer receptive Yin energy. So, how can we achieve this mind-body balance of energy? By cross training with Tai Chi.

The Yin/Yang energy balance is maintained by undertaking a low impact Yin type Tai Chi exercise that is focused on integrating the mind and body, and unifying, and balancing the energy in the body. Tai Chi, therefore, aids relaxation and goes a long way to achieving a more focused mindful awareness, and to achieving peak performance.

Don't forget, not only does this energy balance lead to improved fitness; it also helps to strengthen our immune system which in turn contributes to improving our overall health and wellness.

In improving our overall health Tai Chi supports an athletes desire to improve their performance. This is a very important point, as there are thousands of very fit athletes out there that are not healthy!

What I mean by this is that some athletes are at their peak of fitness but due to pushing themselves to the limit have

Cross Train With Tai Chi

very weak immune systems. These athletes live on the brink of illness or injury as one small cough or cold can have a catastrophic impact on their ability to perform, and all the work undertaken to improve their performance can come crashing down very quickly if their immune system is weak.

One of the many benefits of cross training with Tai Chi is its ability to strengthen the immune system. The good news is that this can be achieved at the same time as the athlete is striving for peak fitness and improved performance.

3. Mind-Body Integration for Peak Performance

3.1 Sports Science and Sports Psychology

Webster's Dictionary defines an athlete as 'one who engages or competes in exercises or games of physical agility, strength, endurance etc.' Cross Training with Tai Chi has a far broader significance and scope.

Aspiring performance athletes tend to focus on physical development, whereas high, or excellent, performers place equal emphasis on developing and integrating both the mind and body. Cross Training with Tai Chi provides the type of physical and mental exercise that enhances the body's awareness and mental focus to improve performance and achieve balance.

Cross training with Tai Chi reinforces that you are a dynamic whole greater than the sum of your parts. Through

Cross Train With Tai Chi

the integration of your mind, body and emotions by cross training with Tai Chi you are able to relax, stay calmer under pressure and deliver results as expected time after time.

Let's now take a look at modern sports science and sports psychology and its coexistence with Tai Chi cross training.

What is Sports Science?

Sports science can be defined as a discipline that studies how the healthy human body works during exercise, and how sport and physical activity promote health from a cellular to whole body perspective.

The study of disciplines such as anatomy, physiology, biomechanics, and psychology as they relate to sporting performance all contribute to the scope and effectiveness of sports science in improving athletic performance, and general health and wellbeing.

Tai Chi includes many of the elements of sports science, particularly those related to postural alignment and structure, building on its relationship with anatomy, physiology, biomechanics and neuroscience. This, coupled with some of the more mindful elements of Sports Psychology, shows that Tai Chi provides a well rounded and developed mind-body cross training exercise that athletes should consider to enhance their personal development and performance.

3. Mind-Body Integration For Peak Performance

What is Sports Psychology?

The American Psychological Association (APA) defines Sports Psychology as a proficiency that uses psychological knowledge and skills to address optimal performance and wellbeing of athletes.

Another more detailed definition is that 'success or failure often depends on mental factors as much as physical ones.' Sports Psychologists recognise the dramatic impact of the athlete's mindset and focus on preparing the mind to overcome obstacles while boosting confidence for optimal performance.

By definition, Sports Psychology is the study of mental factors as they relate to athletes. Sports Psychology is commonly referred to as "sport and exercise psychology," as it is used for team sports as well as individual fitness endeavours.

If we look at this combination of Sports Psychology and Sports Science in the context of Tai Chi, I believe Tai Chi's integrated mind-body exercise system contributes to both sports science and sport psychology objectives and goals, and can lead to improvements in an athlete's performance, particularly in endurance and ball game sports, and will also support an athlete's desire to reduce the likelihood of injury or speed-up a rehabilitation program after injury.

As outlined previously, if we take the example of football or soccer, the pressure to perform at the highest level with the ever increasing media focus and the high expectations of

Cross Train With Tai Chi

the club, from both senior management and the fans, often results in increased stress and anxiety, leading to problems maintaining a high level of performance on the pitch, and can lead to physical injury.

Therefore, cross training with Tai Chi can help us achieve a state of peak performance where actions are relaxed, automatic, intuitive and unconscious, where bursts of 'spontaneous excellence' occur naturally and effortlessly.

In summary, we know that a typical sports science course or training includes:

- Postural alignment

- Anatomy

- Biomechanics

- Physiology

And sports psychology includes:

- Effective Thinking-Skills

- Focused awareness and attention

- Goal Setting

- Imagery and Visualisation

- Stress Management

3. Mind-Body Integration For Peak Performance

As both Sports Science and Sports Psychology are not mutually exclusive it's possible to seek out and cater for their benefits by introducing the athlete to a practical program of Tai Chi mind/body exercise. Chapter 4 outlines a typical training course or program.

Tai Chi supports an athlete's drive to achieve improved results, both in training and in competition, by helping to unite the mind, the body, the breathing and the energy in a far more relaxed way.

A Balanced mind and body leads to Peak Performance

Phrases like peak performance, transcendence, flow and in the zone, all refer to the bursts of spontaneous excellence experienced by top athletes, and describe a state where actions are easy, the focus is 100%, and the athlete knows instinctively what to do to win.

Cross training Tai Chi can, therefore, contribute to the athlete achieving this zone like state, not just every now and then, but more frequently when the mind and body work together in a relaxed manner to support the delivery of excellence.

3.2 Stress and Mindfulness

Stress often results in you forgetting to do or say something. For example, you forget to lock the front door or leave out a

Cross Train With Tai Chi

section of a wedding speech. Depending on the individual the stress of forgetting can make some people very anxious and can lead to mental and bodily health issues.

However, in the main, the human race is very resilient so this lower level stress can easily be addressed without the individual becoming over stressed or anxious.

However, if you're a professional or serious amateur athlete performing in an arena or stadium where thousands of people are watching and shouting positive or negative comments, then your stress levels are likely to be very high, as both your expectations and those of your supporters add to what is already a stressful situation.

This is where cross training with Tai Chi can help. Tai Chi is an exercise that is supported by being able to integrate both thoughts and body movement, supported by effective breathing, which in turn promotes relaxation and a calmer mind.

Mindfulness or being in the present moment is vital if you want to achieve or complete a task not only effectively but also efficiently. Meditation is the ideal practice to become more mindful and also has many benefits to help the mind stay present, sharp and calm. Tai Chi is considered to be a meditative exercise and is often called 'moving meditation'. Its slow continuous coordinated body movements call upon a calm state of mind, just like that achieved while meditating.

64

3. Mind-Body Integration For Peak Performance

Tai Chi, therefore, provides an all round complete mind and body exercise that includes the benefits of meditation practice, such that if you were to practice Tai Chi regularly you may not need to include an additional meditation practice in your training.

Therefore, if you're an athlete in a highly stressed situation and you are cross training with Tai Chi, you can call upon these new found skills to focus on your breathing, relax your body and increase your mindfulness, intention and focused awareness, thus enabling you to perform as required, or expected, on a regular and consistent basis.

3.3 Keeping your Mind Calm with Tai Chi

As we have seen previously, attention to the breath and effective breathing is central to Tai Chi. When your body is relaxed and your breathing is deep, smooth and even, this promotes a calm unified mind-body state that can help support an athlete in achieving their goals. Being able to call upon this calmness of mind brought about through cross training with Tai Chi helps to reduce stress and anxiety before, during and directly after an event or game.

We have now seen how important the integration of both body and mind is if you want to improve your sports performance, or you are in a high-pressure situation i.e. taking

Cross Train With Tai Chi

a penalty in soccer, or serving at match point at Wimbledon.

We have also seen that in mainstream training the mind and body are often tackled as individual mutually exclusive exercises when the real benefits come about when the output is greater than the sum of the two parts, and the mind and body are working together.

Cross training with Tai Chi combines mind and body exercises to ensure the mind and body are integrated. The next section outlines the essential principles, or foundations, necessary to achieve a dynamically relaxed and integrated mind and body.

3.4 Tai Chi Essential Principles

The Ten Essential Principles of Tai Chi were initially organised, developed and communicated by Grandmaster Yang ChengFu (see www.yangfamilytaichi.com for additional information on the history of Tai Chi and Traditional Yang family Tai Chi Chuan) after years of practice and application both from a martial arts and health perspective. These Tai Chi principles are the foundations and building blocks and are fundamental to learning and developing body awareness and your Tai Chi skills.

The Ten Essential Principles can be divided into 3 main areas:

3. Mind-Body Integration For Peak Performance

a). Aligning the Body Frame

1. Head Lifts Up

2. Relax Shoulders and Sink Elbows

3. Chest Relaxed Back Raised

4. Waist Relaxed and Hips Soft.

If the body shape is incorrect you cannot root and connect the upper, middle and lower body to help unify the energy.

b). Coordinating the Motion

5. Empty and Full Clear

6. Upper and Lower Body Connected

7. Continuous Movement

c). Harmonising the Mind

8. Use Mind Intent not Force

9. Internal and External Combined

10. Tranquillity in Movement

Let's take a look at each principle in a little more detail.

Cross Train With Tai Chi

1. **Head Lifts Up** – The Head should be naturally suspended from the Crown Point. Imagine feeling the crown being lifted by a strand of cotton. This allows for a feeling of openness and looseness in the neck vertebrae. Care should be taken not to pull up too much otherwise the neck becomes too tense and you've gone too far. You must have an intention, which is empty, lively (or free) and natural. Without this, you won't be able to raise your spirit.

2. **Relax Shoulders and Sink Elbows** – Sinking the shoulders means the shoulders relax open and hang downward. If you can't relax them downward, the shoulders pop up and the Qi (Chi), or energy follows upward causing the body to become unstable. Dropping or sinking the elbows means the elbows are relaxed downward. If the elbows are elevated above the shoulders then the shoulders cannot relax and hang down.

3. **Chest Relaxed Back Raised** – The phrase 'hold in the chest' means the chest should feel soft and very slightly sunk inward. If you're able to gently sink your chest and your shoulders are down then the upper back will become rounded and rise very slightly, allowing the Qi (Chi) and breath to sink down. If you

3. Mind-Body Integration For Peak Performance

protrude the chest the body becomes 'top heavy' and unstable. Care must be taken so that you don't collapse the chest in an over exaggerated fashion causing improper alignment.

4. **Waist Relaxed Hips Soft** – the waist is the commander or controller of the whole body. Only after you are able to relax the waist will the two legs have strength and the lower body become stable. If the waist is not relaxed and hips are not softened then the upper and lower body cannot connect properly. This, in turn, will mean that the waist will be too slow and cumbersome to direct the energy quickly and directly when required. In Tai Chi terms the waist area also includes the area of the hips and an imaginary band right around the body, incorporating the lower back.

5. **Empty and Full Clear** – to differentiate between substantial (full) and insubstantial (empty), you must clearly differentiate between the leg that is empty of weight and the leg supporting the weight of the body. For example, if the whole body sits on the right leg, then the right leg is deemed 'full' and the left leg 'empty'. If the whole body sits on the left leg, then the left leg is deemed 'full' and the right leg 'empty'. Only after you

are able to distinguish full and empty will turning movements be light, nimble and almost without effort. If you are unable to distinguish them, then your steps will be heavy and sluggish and you're standing unstable.

6. **Upper and Lower Body connected** – in the Tai Chi classics 'Synchronise Upper and Lower Body' is often expressed as follows: 'With the feet rooted in the ground, the energy is developed in the legs, controlled by the waist, manifested through the arms and hands. Only then can we say lower, middle and upper bodies are connected and synchronised. If one part doesn't move then it is not coordinated with the rest of the body.

7. **Continuous Movement** – The movements, 'beginning to end', need to be continuous. Tai Chi uses intent rather than force, and from beginning to end, smoothly and ceaselessly, completes a cycle returning to the beginning while the energy circulates endlessly. That is what the Tai Chi classics refer to when they say 'the movement is like the endlessly flowing Chinese Yangtze or Yellow River.

8. **Use Mind Intent, not Force** – the Tai Chi classics say, 'this is completely a matter of using intent rather

3. Mind-Body Integration For Peak Performance

than force.' When you practice Tai Chi, let the entire body relax and extend. Don't employ even the tiniest amount of stiff strength or tension to cause musculoskeletal or circulatory problems. If you use intent rather than force, then wherever the intent goes the Qi (Chi) follows, and the power comes from the mind and not the muscles. This can be a difficult concept to grasp. How can you develop force without using muscular strength? In Tai Chi, the lower, upper and middle body are connected and pliable, and the force is generated through a relaxed and connected body, and directed by the mind.

9. **Internal and External Combined** – combining the internal mind intention and spirit with the external physical movement harmonises, or combines, the internal and external. Your intent and physical body have to be unified as one. If you have good intent without good body structure and alignment you will struggle to accomplish this essential, resulting in your root, or foundation, being poor. It is, therefore, important that the mind, the body and the breath come into a single focus. The body follows the mind responding effortlessly and without interruption. When the body and the mind are one and there is no

Cross Train With Tai Chi

division between what the mind directs and the instantaneous response in the body. It becomes effortless in its highest form.

10. **Tranquillity in Movement** – in Tai Chi we use a state of quietness or inactivity to help overcome the conscious thinking of movement. Thus enabling a state of calm and peacefulness. A combination of the correct body shape and the mind leading the movement helps lift up the spirit. As the body moves the mind should be calm. This way the Tai Chi movements are natural, the mind is centred and calm, with the eyes and ears alert to everything going on around. This is tranquillity in movement.

These essential principles should be viewed and practiced as one. They are not mutually exclusive. The real benefit comes from the sum of the parts, not each individual principle working alone. However, the beginning student should be able to focus and quickly integrate the first four principles within a few weeks.

Let's take a look at how all the principles work together to enhance a practitioner's Tai Chi.

For example, take the fourth principle: "Relax the waist." When seen from the category of "body shape," it means that we try to avoid sticking out the lower back and buttocks by

3. Mind-Body Integration For Peak Performance

relaxing the waist and hips to enable, or maintain, correct postural alignment.

This principle can also be seen from the point of view of "coordinating the motion," and in particular from a Golf perspective. In Tai Chi, the waist is the controller of all movement. When the waist is relaxed the root is improved and the foundation is stable, resulting in the feet supporting the generation of power.

Movement of the waist on the golfers downward swing connects the lower and upper body and allows for the smooth transfer of power. According to Bobby Jones (professional Golfer), the most important movement in golf is to start the downswing by beginning the unwinding, or turning, of the waist and hips. There can be no effective and efficient power of accuracy in golf unless a relaxed waist leads the downswing, and the foundation, or stance, is stable or rooted.

If we now take a look from a martial arts perspective, without a relaxed waist, it will be difficult to yield and/or evade your opponent's force and energy while remaining rooted or grounded to the floor. Without an adequate root, just as in a tree, the tree or person can be easily uprooted or toppled over.

From the "mind/spirit" perspective, relaxing the waist allows for the breath to deepen and the Qi (Chi) to sink, which helps to calm and clear the mind.

73

Cross Train With Tai Chi

A typical Tai Chi program of learning should be built on the Ten Essential Principles, and also include specific exercises to help improve the students understanding and 'feeling awareness' when practiced correctly.

3.5 In the Zone

Let's talk about the state of flow initially. Flow is a state of effortless concentration that results from a period of intense focus. It is often seen and talked about as some form of sports enlightenment. Athletes report being in a state of flow, or in the zone, during their best performances.

Being in the zone or flow begins at the point that focus stops becoming difficult and starts becoming easy. Entering a state of flow requires justified self-confidence, unforced concentration, relaxation, alertness and a positive attitude. Often the enemies of flow, or being in the zone, are the desire to win, the desire to impress others, an excessive non-relaxed effort to achieve a state of flow, and lack of initiative.

Phrases like peak performance, transcendence and in the zone, all refer to the bursts of spontaneous excellence experienced by top athletes, and describe a state where their actions become easy, the focus is 100% and the player knows instinctively and intuitively what to do next to succeed.

3. Mind-Body Integration For Peak Performance

Cross training with Tai Chi should lead to an athlete being in the zone more frequently, as Tai Chi exercise and its fundamental principles encourage the body to relax and the mind to become focused and calm.

Tai Chi and the related mind, breath and bodywork provide the athlete with a framework to achieve improved performance while undertaking it in a dynamically relaxed 'flow like' state.

Don't worry if you haven't experienced this flow like state in your training or in competition just yet. By enrolling in a well balanced Tai Chi program (as outlined in chapter 4) you will be well on your way to feeling this desired zone-like state.

4. A Tai Chi Training Program

4.1 Face-to-Face or Online Course?

Most teachers, including Tai Chi Grandmaster Yang ChengFu and his senior student Professor Cheng Man Ching, said finding a good teacher, perseverance and regular practice are vital to developing the skills necessary to improve your performance, especially in sports. Tai Chi is no different; these three elements are fundamental to learning and developing your Tai Chi knowledge and skills.

If you want to become proficient, or the best, in anything you do, it's no good practicing and persevering with a poor teacher as your Tai Chi will be built on poor foundations and we all know what happens to any structure built on poor foundations!

However, it's also not ideal if you have a great teacher but rarely practice, as your Tai Chi skills, are unlikely to develop

Cross Train With Tai Chi

as expected and it will take your body and mind a lot longer to learn and replicate your new found skills. This, therefore, confirms the old adage you only get out what you put in. Ask any athlete or their coach, and they will say your ability to learn and develop your skill is directly proportional to the deliberate or purposeful practice undertaken.

What does deliberate practice mean? Ericsson in his book 'Peak – Secrets from the New Science of Expertise' states that non-focused practice and the idea that 10,000 hours of practice leads to mastery, is incorrect. To become extremely proficient you need to practice deliberately and purposely. This is not just practicing what you learned last week in class. This is a more focused personal approach, led by an expert teacher, to achieve your performance goals. The importance of deliberate practice is explained in more detail in section 5.1.

We now understand that a very good teacher or instructor is fundamental to effective learning, but excellent teaching alone is not enough. As the saying goes the teacher can lead the horse (or athlete in this case) to water, but they can't make it drink it – or again, in our case can't make the student practice. The student needs to practice deliberately and with perseverance to become the best they can be.

4. A Tai Chi Training Program

How do you find a Good Teacher?

Finding a good teacher is often an onerous research activity and several of the following need to be considered before choosing a Tai Chi teacher.

- Identify classes that are relatively close to you. How close is a personal thing based on a teacher meeting your expectations, your practical travel constraints, and the cost to attend a class?

- Research the prospective teachers Tai Chi website, as this will give you information on the type or style of Tai Chi practiced, how long the teacher has been practicing and teaching, and who they have learned, and continue to learn from. Be aware that on the Internet teachers can portray themselves in whatever way they want. You really need to get answers to the questions:

- Are they still learning?

- Do they still attend seminars and classes with their masters/teachers?

- Do they belong to an accredited and well-known International Association, or are they going it alone?

Cross Train With Tai Chi

- Check out several local Tai Chi classes to get a feel for the class, particularly whether the style of teaching and the personality of the teacher is accommodating.

- When attending a class check out the teacher's style and demeanour, and interact with, and if possible, seek feedback from other students

- All things being equal an experienced teacher, one that has been teaching a long time is more likely to teach more practically and effectively. An experienced teacher should be very familiar and embody the Tai Chi principles and exercises that he or she teaches and be able to guide you to the deeper aspects of Tai Chi

- Try to find out if the teacher has long-standing students? These are students who have been studying with the teacher for over 5 years. This commitment reflects well, on the teacher.

- If the teacher has good teaching and people skills he or she is able to maximise the learning of not just a group of students but also bring out the best in an individual student. A word of warning here, though. As outlined above, a student who does not practice regularly and often (e.g. ideally 10-15 minutes per day) will not reap the benefits of their teacher's instruction and coaching

4. A Tai Chi Training Program

as quickly as new students who practice often but with average teachers.

Tai Chi Online

I would like to be very clear here, Face-to-Face classroom type training with a very good Tai Chi teacher is always the best and the ideal way forward. However, average or poorly experienced Face to Face Tai Chi teachers may well cause injury, result in poor structural alignment and stunt your learning and development.

There is another option however; this option is to learn Tai Chi via an online Tai Chi program or course. A few years back I would not have recommended any online programs or courses. However, with the introduction of various online teaching frameworks and tools that include presentations, video, and one-to-one feedback, through online membership programs, it is now much easier to provide extra value when giving corrective feedback to the student, as long as the student is prepared to take on board the feedback and continue to practice and persevere.

Online video programs with a personalised 1:1 service are very good nowadays, as they provide the knowledge and expertise to enable those students who do not have access to a local Tai Chi class nearby, or cannot travel, to learn from a very experienced teacher online. These online courses

Cross Train With Tai Chi

provide teachers with the ability to show video footage of moves from various positions to enable effective student learning.

This approach is more flexible as the student can study and practice in their own time and at their own pace, and maybe attend group and/or 'one on one' sessions with the teacher to further develop their skills and knowledge.

In today's highly stressed work and home environment online courses and teaching are becoming the number one approach to learning. Cross training with Tai Chi online can provide the student, particularly the beginner, with the resources and a flexible approach to Tai Chi that an athlete and cross trainer requires.

Whilst there are downsides to online training, such as the teacher's ability to actively correct a student's moves through physical touch, many students do not like to be touched so this part of the normal face to face training would not be welcomed anyway.

In summary, your normal Tai Chi face-to-face classes encourage student interaction and questioning. The question and answer sessions tend to benefit the whole class even if you are someone who does not like to ask questions. Online learning calls for a more dedicated individualistic approach to learning and regular daily practice. Online learning does provide those students who prefer a more, one on one direct

4. A Tai Chi Training Program

approach to learning with an opportunity to ask questions and receive personal feedback on their progress. The analysis and study of videos showing the student practicing can help achieve this.

Both approaches work and can be delivered well when the student commits and decides which type of learning meets their needs. Another hybrid approach is to combine the two, where a student may base his or her primary learning online and also attend face-to-face seminars with their online teacher. This approach allows the student to meet their teacher, ask questions and receive hands-on correction and feedback to further enhance their skills and develop the student teacher relationship.

It is not recommended that the student train with two different teachers, one at a local class and another online. Students should seek out a consistent approach to their instruction otherwise the student may become confused.

However, there is one exception to this and that is where the primary teacher has a senior student who is now an instructor. This person can provide similar instruction and coaching as the primary teacher as they have been trained using the same or very similar methods and associated feedback mechanisms.

If you are interested in learning more from a certified teacher with 18 plus years of Tai Chi experience, go to

Cross Train With Tai Chi

www.taichicrosstraining.com to express an interest in my forthcoming online course.

4.2 An Example Training Program

A typical Tai Chi program needs to be both pragmatic and supportive of the athlete's primary sports training. An overview of a typical Tai Chi exercise program is shown below.

- Warm-Up and Stretching, including joint mobility exercises

- Mindful lower abdominal breathing

- Wu Chi Postural alignment (This posture enables the student to feel and directly experience the first four 10 essential principles – see section 3.4)

- Learning the Traditional Yang family Hand form

- Visualisation and imagery

- Bodywork: Feeling Awareness and sensitivity training. Where you differentiate between thoughts, feelings and directly experiencing increased body sensitivity.

These core program components can be integrated into a weekly or monthly training schedule to enable the student to

4. A Tai Chi Training Program

learn and practice in a coordinated and effective manner so as to maximise the student's benefits.

4.3 A Typical Training Course

When practicing Tai Chi, there are two main goals to keep in mind:

- To be rooted, balanced, and stable, both in mind and body

- To unify the energy of the whole body

How can we be stable and rooted? By implementing the Ten Essential principles, particularly the first four principles. These are very much focused on relaxing the body and adopting the correct postural alignment. When combined with abdominal deep breathing this helps to sink the Qi (Chi) and strengthen your root.

When the upper body feels light, the lower body heavy, and the middle body (waist and hips) relaxed and soft, you are able to improve your root, connect the whole body, and unify the energy flow throughout the body.

As stated previously, this relaxed state is often referred to in Tai Chi as being 'Sung.' In achieving this relaxed state we are effectively loosening and extending the tendons and ligaments

Cross Train With Tai Chi

through the joints. This type of relaxation is often referred to as dynamic relaxation and is a fundamental mind-body state that the Tai Chi student aims to achieve. This same dynamic relaxed state is also something that all athletes would benefit from, as a relaxed and calmly focused athlete is more likely to perform better than a tense and anxious athlete.

An online course should, therefore, provide theoretical and practical learning of the essential principles in conjunction with the relevant mind and body exercises required to achieve both goals above.

Let's take a look at the content of a typical 'Tai Chi Cross Training' course module. This first module will cover both theoretical and practical learning and requires the student to practice diligently throughout the month.

The module objectives are to:

- Review the benefits of Tai Chi Cross Training

- Outline the fundamental learning opportunities of the whole course

- Learn some basic movements

- Reinforce the importance of deliberate regular daily practice.

Let us now look at the first module in a little more detail:

4. A Tai Chi Training Program

Module 1 – Principles and Practice

1.1 Tai Chi Course benefits and objectives

- Benefits and objectives

- Fundamental learning:

- Course Book: 'Cross Training with Tai Chi' (this book)

- Yin/Yang Philosophy and the Ten Essential principles

- Link to various sports

- Imagery and Visualisation

- Breathing and relaxation

- Body and feeling awareness

- Sensitivity and direct experience

- Mindfulness and meditation

- Neuroscience and importance of mind-body connection

- First steps

- Warm-Up and Stretching exercises

Cross Train With Tai Chi

- Bodywork and feeling awareness

- Standing Pole Meditation

- 'Grasp the Birds Tail' and 'Single Whip' form movements

- Learning and adopting the four alignment principles to help build the foundations of your Tai Chi skills

1.2 Relaxation and the 10 essential principles

- Relaxation in the context of Tai Chi

- Explain the ten essentials and how important the first four body postural structure/alignment principles are when starting your practice

- Provide examples of 'feeling awareness' and 'sensitivity' based on these four key principles

1.3 Videos and detailed instruction (including photos)

- Wu Chi posture and body alignment characteristics

- 5 points of practice description

- Bow and Empty stances

4. A Tai Chi Training Program

- Hand shape

- Preparation and Beginning form

- Left and Right ward-off

- Taster for Module 2

- Show typical errors and how to correct

- Application/Method

1.4 Practice before the next Module or Session

- 10-15 minutes practice every day

- Perseverance, practice, and patience

- Further training: Online Modular Course

- Mod 1 – Principles and Practice (this module)

- Mod 2 – Theory and Form

- Mod 3 – Form and Practice

- Mod 4 – Posture and Relaxation

- Mod 5 – Mindfulness, Patience and Perseverance

Cross Train With Tai Chi

- Mod 6 – Course Completion and Next Steps

Each of these modules contains a series of Tai Chi Hand Form movements. The supportive video footage shown in each module is provided to:

- Show the student the sequence of Tai Chi moves and thereby provide them with an aide memoir and other resources they need to help complete the course.

- Support student learning. It does not in any way replace the need for an effective face-to-face or online teacher.

Resources to be made available to students when they enrol in my planned online course include:

- Online program membership and personal training

- Access to Tai Chi Hand form videos

- Student Handbook

- 'Cross Train with Tai Chi' book

- Excel training plan and Ten Essential Principles checklist

Don't forget to go to **www.taichicrosstraining.com** to express an interest in my forthcoming online course.

5. How Do I know it's Working?

5.1 Deliberate Practice and Managing your Expectations

Let's assume you want to cross train with Tai Chi as you now feel it can offer you that whole body and mind exercise system to help you improve your performance as an athlete and bring about a new sense of calmness in your daily life.

Before moving on let's revisit some of the key benefits of cross training with Tai Chi.

Tai Chi is a well rounded low impact stress-free exercise that helps you maintain mind-body balance, both during and after exercise, and keeps you motivated, excited, and in good shape.

Studies have shown that Tai Chi helps to strengthen bone density and the immune system resulting in improved health and overall wellness, and prevents overuse injuries, or

Cross Train With Tai Chi

supports the athlete regaining physical balance and leg strength after an injury.

If you need to rehabilitate from an injury, such as muscle pulls, strains, or tears, Tai Chi provides the kind of exercise that allows you to stay in shape and lets your body heal while you exercise.

Tai Chi provides a level of focused attention and awareness that when combined with effective and deliberate practice can lead to enhanced performance.

Musculoskeletal strength, flexibility, neuromuscular coordination, and reflexes are all improved when practicing Tai Chi.

The slow coordinated exercise routines of Tai Chi help to balance out both sides of the body.

Tai Chi offers many pluses to raise the level of your game. It provides flexibility, balance, strength and modest conditioning of both body and mind.

All athletes can benefit from applying many of the ingredients of Tai Chi, including intention, deep breathing, integrated movement, and moderation.

The deepened mind-body connection Tai Chi affords can help you see each movement of your chosen sport exactly as you would like it to be.

Tai Chi abdominal breathing (or belly breathing) can be used as a tool for relaxation; a relaxed athlete is a more efficient,

5. How Do I know it's Working?

better-coordinated athlete. Relaxation helps to eliminate tension, stress, and anxiety, all of which can impede performance.

Tai Chi deep breathing helps lower your heart rate, relax your muscles, increase your mind-body connection, raise your confidence levels, and create a calm, focused state of mind. Especially in high-pressure moments (e.g. taking a penalty kick in soccer, standing on the first Tee in golf, or at set or match point in tennis).

Using numerous Tai Chi techniques can help you "get in the zone" while playing any sport.

Tai Chi can improve your overall health by balancing cardio type training with low impact body and mind training.

It's well known that you get the greatest athletic benefit from training your neurological system. Tai Chi uses unfamiliar movement patterns to strengthen your neurological system, which in turn improves your coordination, balance, stability, grace and alignment.

For more serious, and more technical sports specific requirements, Tai Chi offers a strategic approach to exercise where enhanced performance can be obtained by varying your exercise schedule to develop specific skills or mindset.

Based on these benefits and a better understanding of how and why cross training with Tai Chi could become the type of cross training you need, let's have a look at your expectations and how these can be realised with a practical

Cross Train With Tai Chi

and pragmatic Tai Chi course that supports a more balanced mind-body approach to your training.

My soon to launched online course emphasises a clearly focused Tai Chi exercise system that is built on excellent teaching, deliberate practice and perseverance.

Before I continue, let's revisit 'Deliberate Practice' – What do we mean by deliberate practice? According to Anders Ericsson, in his highly regarded book 'PEAK: Secrets from the New Science of Expertise', deliberate or purposeful practice is key to seeking out steady and lasting improvement in anything we do. Ericsson argues that heartfelt desire and hard work alone are not enough. It is the right sort of deliberate practice carried out over a significant period of time that leads to considerable improvement. The details about the 'right sort of practice' are drawn from the relatively new area of Psychology that can best be described as 'the science of expertise'.

To learn any new skill or gain expertise you need to practice, practice, practice. There isn't much debate about that. But here's what you might not know: scientific research shows that the quality of your practice is just as important as the quantity. Ericsson argues that it's not about what natural talent you're born with. It's about how consistently and deliberately you can work to improve your performance.

Deliberate practice is a structured activity engaged in with

5. How Do I know it's Working?

the specific goal of improving performance. When you engage in deliberate practice, improving your performance over time is your goal and motivation. Cross Training with Tai Chi allows the athlete to rethink their training program and integrate a deliberate Tai Chi practice in their routine.

Anders Ericsson, outlines four essential components of deliberate practice, as follows:

1. You must be motivated to attend to the task and exert effort to improve your performance.

2. The design of the task should take into account your pre-existing knowledge so that the task can be correctly understood after a brief period of instruction.

3. You should receive immediate informative feedback and knowledge of results of your performance.

4. You should repeatedly perform the same or similar tasks.

When these conditions are met, practice improves accuracy and speed of performance on cognitive, perceptual, and motor tasks. Ericsson states, 'simply practice alone isn't enough to rapidly gain skills. Mere repetition of an activity won't lead to improved performance. Your practice must be intentional, aimed at improving performance, designed for

Cross Train With Tai Chi

your current skill level and combined with immediate feedback and repetition.'

It's important to note that without receiving adequate feedback on your performance during practice, then efficient and effective learning is impossible and improvement is minimal. The role of the Tai Chi teacher or instructor, whether in class or online, cannot be overstated to ensure deliberate practice is in place and being adhered too.

With a deliberate practice framework in place, you can start to manage your expectations. This is especially important when starting something new, as we normally set our expectations way too high.

My advice is to start slowly and create a weekly learning and practice schedule that you can manage in what is probably a pretty busy lifestyle. Persevere with this schedule throughout the first 6 months of your Tai Chi study to lay the foundations to realising the benefits and personal improvement expected.

Remember, don't push yourself to learn too quickly.

- Don't just 'wedge-in' more exercise to an already busy training schedule. Cross training with Tai Chi should lead to you cancelling or suspending some of your current primary sports sessions to accommodate and achieve a more balanced practice.

5. How Do I know it's Working?

- Make your Tai Chi training inclusive of your primary sport exercise sessions so that it forms part of your overall weekly exercise regime.

- Additional Tai Chi sessions can be added when you are recovering from an injury or feel particularly anxious or stressed out.

- Review the forthcoming week's schedule to see if minor changes in your primary sports sessions can accommodate your more relaxed and mindful Tai Chi session(s).

- Do not take on too much, as you want to feel relaxed and energised after a Tai Chi session, in readiness for becoming more focused on your primary sports training and competition.

In summary, having a pragmatic approach to introducing Tai Chi into your already busy exercise schedule should reduce your expectation levels and allow you to relax into your new Tai Chi sessions using the 70% moderation rule.

Try not to rush in and treat this exercise as a new fad. Try to treat the learning and practice as an adventure. With consistent deliberate practice and perseverance, you will reap the benefits and become a calmer person ready to take that next step to achieve your personal goals while improving your overall health and wellness.

Cross Train With Tai Chi

Remember the famous saying 'You can't build Rome in a day.' Please keep this in mind, as the benefits of cross training with Tai Chi will only be fully realised over time.

Let's now take a look at how you can measure and track your progress along the way.

5.2 Tracking Progress

Tracking your progress, particularly your daily practice is vital if you want to realise the benefits of your Tai Chi cross training. Having a training schedule and maintaining a log of your practice keeps you focused and on track. If the training log also includes areas for recording comments on how you are progressing, then even better. This way you are more likely to stick to the plan or schedule as you track your progress and achievement.

Journaling your progress enables you to record the positive aspects of how well your training is going each week, and also helps you identify areas that you may be struggling with or where progress is slow. You can then address the relevant exercises and Tai Chi moves that you are struggling to understand, or having some difficulty carrying out, through discussion with your teacher. This will enable your teacher to answer any questions or issues you may have and also guide you in your practice. This should result in your teacher providing

5. How Do I know it's Working?

greater clarity, and maybe, including additional bodywork exercises to ensure your learning and progress remains on track.

To help Tai Chi cross training students track their progress I have produced a 'Weekly Tai Chi Log (Microsoft Excel format).' Students who purchase this book or visit my download page at www.taichicrosstraining.com can download the log absolutely free.

This Log can be utilised as soon as you have started your face-to-face class or online Tai Chi course. Alternatively, you could create your own log or supplement your current primary sports plan and log with Tai Chi exercises. I would recommend your log include the following sections and items:

Warm Up and Stretching

- Hand Tapping Body Massage

- Major joint warm-up exercises (neck, shoulders, elbows, wrist, hips, knees and ankles)

- Stretching (calves, hamstrings, quads, groin, etc)

Tai Chi Body/Mind Work

- Standing Pole Meditation

- Waist/arm connection exercises

- Loosening and opening joint exercises

Cross Train With Tai Chi

- Wu Chi (or preparation) stance

- 4 Key Postural alignment principles

Tai Chi Hand Form

- Bow and Empty stance line walking

- Preparation

- Beginning form

- Moves 1 to 3

- Moves 4 – 6

- Moves 7 – 12

- Moves 13 – 16

- 1st section of Form (moves 1 – 16)

Reading and Research

- This book

- Essential Tai Chi Chuan Student Handbook

- Author's Tai Chi Website
  www.taichicrosstraining.com

- Internet and book resources (see chapter 6)

5. How Do I know it's Working?

Progress Achievement

- Did you complete your daily weekly practice?

- Mark yourself out of 10 for sticking with your week's plan

- Number of practice sessions this week (approximate number of minutes practiced each day and week)

Comments

- How did the week go?

- Have you met your objectives?

- What did you hope to learn and accomplish?

- Did you achieve this?

- What went well?

- What did you have trouble with, if any?

- Areas for discussion with your teacher

5.3 Is it Working?

How do you know cross training with Tai Chi is working for you?

This can be a difficult question to answer. As you will need to have recorded your performance before you start to cross train with Tai Chi, and then set clear measurable goals

Cross Train With Tai Chi

and targets that you would expect to achieve after completing a Tai Chi course.

Is this really feasible and relevant? Probably not, as there are a number of intangible Tai Chi benefits, which are a little more difficult to measure. Maybe in the business world, and particularly when measuring the delivery timescales of a product, or measuring improvements in customer service, this method of measuring your progress or knowing if all the improvement actions have led to realising the benefits expected is feasible.

However, cross training with Tai Chi cannot be adequately measured this way. For example, one of the benefits of cross training with Tai Chi is to achieve a calmer and more relaxed persona so that you can deal with stressful or anxious situations, both in your training and in competition. How do we measure this? This is very subjective and will vary by individual. Maybe we need to look for changes in the athlete's primary sports performance and health.

Some changes the athlete may notice are:

• More consistent performance

• Performance improvement from month three of the Tai Chi class or course

5. How Do I know it's Working?

- Feeling more healthy and less tired

- Having fewer injuries or illnesses

So, where do we go from here? How will you know if cross training with Tai Chi is working?

One way is to create some form of feedback mechanism or method where students answer a number of tangible and intangible questions, that when answered honestly provide a very good indication of how cross training with Tai Chi is helping them to become a more relaxed, and consistent performer.

The feedback questionnaire below was created to provide the student with an opportunity to identify if cross training with Tai Chi is actually working for them. This feedback should only be completed after a minimum of 3 months Tai Chi training and practice, as after this period of time a number of benefits can, and should, be realised. This, of course, assumes the student has practiced regularly, ideally 10 to 15 minutes per day. This feedback review can then be repeated after 6 months to compare results.

Cross Train With Tai Chi

Feedback Questionnaire

1. Have you been Tai Chi training for at least 3 months?

2. Have you been going to classes or following an online program or course?

3. Are you practicing at least 10 minutes per day?

4. Do you feel less tired and irritable?

5. Do you feel more energised after a Tai Chi session?

6. Do friends and family notice a change in you? Are you a more relaxed calmer person?

7. Do you feel sharper and more in control?

8. Are you able to breathe deeper and longer now?

9. Has deeper breathing helped you to achieve a calmer and focused mind?

10. Has deeper breathing helped you to achieve a more relaxed body?

11. Has your performance in your primary sport improved? Or at least become more consistent?

5. How Do I know it's Working?

12. Are you feeling healthier?

13. Have you had fewer colds or illnesses since starting your Tai Chi training?

14. Have you suffered fewer injuries?

15. If recuperating from injury, have you noticed that your normal recovery time has reduced, and you can return to your primary sport earlier?

16. Is it a little easier for you to relax and calm your mind and body during high-intensity training sessions, or when competing, since you have been cross training with Tai Chi?

Analysing the Results

We can now analyse the results by counting the number of questions answered 'Yes.' The following conclusions can probably be made.

If you answered 'Yes' to 10 or more questions, then:

Cross training with Tai Chi is significantly contributing to improving your performance, health and overall physical and mental wellness – Keep up the excellent work, continue with the course or program to sustain and enhance your early benefits.

Cross Train With Tai Chi

If you answered 'Yes' to more than 4 but less than 10 questions, then:

Keep going with your Tai Chi cross training as you have made good progress. Remember, some people take to new exercises or tasks better than others so an individual's progress can vary considerably even when undertaking the same class or course.

Going forwards, continue to ask your teacher additional questions to help improve your understanding. This way you will be getting a little more personal feedback on how and what to practice to enable you to make those subtle body and mind corrections. This, in turn, should lead to improving and developing your Tai Chi skills, improving your primary sports performance and overall health and wellness. Your learning and practice will then become far more focused and deliberate, rather than just repeating a move or exercise over and over in an incorrect manner.

If you answered 'Yes' to fewer than 4 questions, then:

I'm sure you will be questioning if cross training with Tai Chi is really for working for you. At this point you may want to review those questions you said 'Yes' to, as you may feel that you have gained a significant benefit in just answering 'Yes' to two questions. For example, just being more relaxed or being able to breathe much deeper has given you the tools to

5. How Do I know it's Working?

develop your ability to relax when under pressure in your primary sport.

Please note; this shows that not all questions carry the same weight or importance. You may decide that just answering 1 or 2 questions with a 'Yes' is positive feedback, as your Tai Chi training is providing you with exactly the results you need and expect. Maybe your health has improved, or you now have a more balanced and energised lifestyle, allowing you to 'push on' and train harder to achieve your primary sports goals.

Alternatively, you may not have given the course or class a chance.

• Did you really follow the course and practice for a minimum of 10 minutes per day? If not, the benefits and the corresponding results are probably as expected, and not a shock to you.

• Do you really understand what is being taught?

• Are you struggling with coordinating the slow even paced movements?

If so, discuss any issues and seek out answers, and helpful hints and tips, from your teacher.

As you can see, all is not lost. You now have the chance to re-work your exercise schedule and refocus your Tai Chi

Cross Train With Tai Chi

training so that the additional benefits can be realised if you persevere with your deliberate daily Tai Chi practice.

Class or Online Course Feedback

Okay, what next? Will you be continuing with your Tai Chi training by integrating it into your training schedule going forward? Would you benefit from a more enhanced form of personal learning, such as 'one to one' with your teacher?

Take a look at some typical course or class feedback questions below. Completing this feedback may help you decide on how you want to progress your Tai Chi cross training going forward.

- Did the class or online course meet your needs?

- Has it helped improve your performance? If not, why do you think this is?

- What could be done to improve the class/course?

- Did the course content meet your expectations?

- Are you looking to carry on your Tai Chi training to make it an integral part of your training?

- What would you like to see added or improved upon?

5. How Do I know it's Working?

- Do you want to further develop and deepen your Tai Chi skills? If so, would you consider continuing your online learning?

- Would you consider a more personal 'one on one' mode of learning, either online or face-to-face with your teacher?

- Would you consider joining an individually focused online membership program? Where you will work directly with your teacher and receive additional, enhanced instruction and feedback?

5.4 Next Steps

This brings me to the end of the book, and if you've stayed with me thus far I would like to thank you for purchasing and reading this book. Hopefully, you have found the content both interesting and thought provoking, and may now be tempted to cross train with Tai Chi to improve your primary sports performance and live a more balanced and healthy life.

If you do decide to enrol in a local Tai Chi class or online course, I'm sure that if you practice regularly and diligently you will not only enjoy this new integrated mind and body training but also feel calmer, healthier, and on your way to

Cross Train With Tai Chi

improving your primary sports performance and achieving your goals.

Don't forget, you can get my free Tai Chi Cross Training Log and access YouTube videos of Grandmaster Yang Jun performing the Yang family Tai Chi Hand Form at **www.taichicrosstraining.com**

And remember; if you're interested in receiving more information, and would like to express an interest in my 'Cross Training with Tai Chi' online course, please go to **www.taichicrosstraining.com**.

6. Resources

A list of recommended resources is shown below.

Internet

See my book website **www.taichicrosstraining.com**

International Yang Family Association
www.yangfamilytaichi.com

Free online resources at **www.taichicrosstraining.com**

Online Course at **www.taichicrosstraining.com**

Finding a UK Teacher – Tai Chi Finder,
www.taichifinder.co.uk

Cross Train With Tai Chi

Books

Gallwey, W.Timothy. *The Inner Game of Tennis*

Kaptchuk, Ted J. Chinese Medicine – *The Web that has no Weaver*

Milman, Dan. *Body Mind Mastery*

Ralston, Peter. *Zen Body Being: An Enlightened Approach to Physical Skill, Grace, and Power*

Liao Waysun, *The Essence of Tai Chi*

Yang, Jun. *Essential Tai Chi Chuan Handbook* (from the International Yang Family Association www.yangfamilytaichi.com)

Wile, Douglas, *Lost T'ai-chi Classics from the Late Ch'ing Dynasty* (Chinese Philosophy and Culture).

Frantzis, Bruce Kumar (2008). *The Chi Revolution: Harnessing the Healing Power of Your Life Force.*

Ericsson Anders and Pool Robert. *PEAK: Secrets from the New Science of Expertise*

6. Resources

Articles

Deng, Y (2003). "Ration of Qi with Modern Essential on Traditional Chinese Medicine Qi: Qi Set, Qi Element". Journal of Mathematical Medicine (in Chinese) 16 (4): 346-347.

About the Author

I am the UK Director and lead certified instructor of the Traditional Yang family Tai Chi Chuan International Association. Having established a successful following in the UK, albeit on a part-time basis, I recently left a management position in the corporate business world to follow my passion and teach Tai Chi full time.

After studying martial arts (Karate) in my late teens, I then went onto have a successful sporting career as a semi-professional soccer player throughout my twenties and early thirties.

I started learning and practicing Tai Chi Chuan in March 1998 and studied with a number of leading Tai Chi masters including Grandmaster Yang ZhenDuo and Grandmaster Yang Jun (5th generation Yang family Tai Chi Chuan current lineage holder).

After my initial studies and research into Tai Chi Chuan, I decided to focus my studies on Traditional Yang Family Tai Chi Chuan with Grandmaster Yang Jun.

I have been teaching the full Yang family Tai Chi Chuan curriculum for approximately 14 years, and I'm a full instructor member of the Tai Chi Union for Great Britain (TCUGB).

I qualified as "Tuina" (Traditional Chinese Medicine) Massage therapist in 2003.

How to contact me

Mike Taylor, (UK Director and Lead Instructor)

miketaichi@gmail.com

www.taichicrosstraining.com

17564587R00072

Printed in Poland
by Amazon Fulfillment
Poland Sp. z o.o., Wrocław

Home

Tonight, it's as if the rain was told
        to wash away all
but the unwrapped gold of evening.
The heavens blush a sudden carmine,
        last leg now, traffic thinning
and the wet world unrolled.
Does solitude brighten this? Is it sweeter
        now I've told you?
There's a ripe pear on the seat beside me.
I have a life, the lit sky, and the pink
        ribbon road home.

Vanessa Lampert

Great Things Have Happened

We were talking about the great things
that have happened in our lifetimes;
and I said, 'Oh, I suppose the moon landing
was the greatest thing that has happened
in my time.' But, of course, we were all lying.
The truth is the moon landing didn't mean
one-tenth as much to me as one night in 1963
when we lived in a three-room flat in what once had been
the mansion of some Victorian merchant prince
(our kitchen had been a clothes closet, I'm sure),
on a street where by now nobody lived
who could afford to live anywhere else.
That night, the three of us, Claudine, Johnnie and me,
woke up at half-past four in the morning
and ate cinnamon toast together.

'Is that all?' I hear somebody ask.

Oh, but we were silly with sleepiness
and, under our windows, the street-cleaners
were working their machines and conversing in Italian, and
everything was strange without being threatening,
even the tea-kettle whistled differently
than in the daytime: it was like the feeling
you get sometimes in a country you've never visited
before, when the bread doesn't taste quite the same,
the butter is a small adventure, and they put
paprika on the table instead of pepper,
except that there was nobody in this country
except the three of us, half-tipsy with the wonder
of being alive, and wholly enveloped in love.

Alden Nowlan (1933 – 1983)

Wood Song

I heard a wood-thrush in the dusk
   Twirl three notes and make a star –
My heart that walked with bitterness
   Came back from very far.

Three shining notes were all he had,
   And yet they made a starry call –
I caught life back against my breast
   And kissed it, scars and all.

Sara Teasdale (1884 – 1933)

Symbiosis

I've seen a horse
take the soft folds of a dog's scruff
between her corn kernel teeth.

He, quite forgetting the bones of himself,
dangled some seconds
before being lowered down.

The care of that horse
as if she were practised in placing
chandeliers, or weighing sacks of truffles
with her mouth

and how the dog paused
as if to reassure the horse
of no awkwardness between them
after that solemn transaction of theirs

in which (I like to think)
no liberties were taken
save a horse who wished
a moment's velvet on her grassy tongue,
an old dog's wish to float.

Em Gray

Delphiniums in a Window Box

Every sunrise, sometimes strangers' eyes.
Not necessarily swans, even crows,
even the evening fusillade of bats.
That place where the creek goes underground,
how many weeks before I see you again?
Stacks of books, every page, character's
rage and poet's strange contraption
of syntax and song, every song
even when there isn't one.
Every thistle, splinter, butterfly
over the drainage ditches. Every stray.
Did you see the meteor shower?
Every question, conversation
even with almost nothing, cricket, cloud,
because of you I'm talking to crickets, clouds,
confiding in a cat. Everyone says
Come to your senses, and I do, of you.
Every touch electric, every taste you,
every smell, even burning sugar, every
cry and laugh. Toothpicked samples
at the farmer's market, every melon,
plum, I come undone, undone.

Dean Young

Cardiologist

For the first time I am raking
the intimate garden

of what is inside me, aorta
and brine, the screen

revealing how much goes
unnoticed, what I have

cheated myself to ignore.
My parents listen

to palpitations,
whispers

from the underground brook
they once discovered

together as newlyweds,
willing it to persevere

past their lifetimes. How strangely
comforting their frenzy at the clinic,

after hearing of misaligned heartbeats
and stress. Such is a responsibility I may

never allow myself to understand:
no less than twenty-two years

in tending cuts, sprains, bruises
or midnight anxieties. Today

I am just like any other
careless child, as I have

always been, with four
palms to kiss when I fall.

Jerrold Yam

Yoga

I think of us two showing off
like the sun shone out of us

lifting your whole body on my feet:
no Gem! Look, look at me!

then suddenly we'd connect
and be still

and later we'd be waitresses
holding boards of little plates

and expensive bowls
and heavy trays

we'd hold up grown men
and hold up whole houses

so in that icy studio where no one looked over
and not knowing what to do with block or strap

I imagined the mat as that patch of summer grass
you holding the dog so she didn't get squashed

me wobbling and kicking one leg to meet the other
        you shouting *nearly nearly – yes you've got it, go on!*

Laurie Bolger

The Way Water Shapes a Landscape

These are the first moments of the day:
one pillow under your head,
the other in your arms
and you are in this slash of light,
your slopes of skin buzzing with lost hormones.

Outside, the sun scratches furrows up the crags,
a blackbird anxiously practises two phrases

and inside you are about to invent a feasible day.
How does the miracle occur?

In the shower you are still no more
than a spinal column topped by
a roundish ball of memories.
The water taps and taps at you
like a patient sculptor
and then

there now
that's you in the mirror, behind the steam;
this is you, dear stranger,
tying on your bones, your strung muscles.

Paula Jennings (1950 – 2024)

Meditations in an Emergency

I wake up & it breaks my heart. I draw the blinds & the thrill of rain breaks my heart. I go outside. I ride the train, walk among the buildings, men in Monday suits. The flight of doves, the city of tents beneath the underpass, the huddled mass, old women hawking roses, & children all of them, break my heart. There's a dream I have in which I love the world. I run from end to end like fingers through her hair. There are no borders, only wind. Like you, I was born. Like you, I was raised in the institution of dreaming. Hand on my heart. Hand on my stupid heart.

Cameron Awkward-Rich

Swallows

Every day or two I message Joanna
and every day or two she replies.
We never meet but we talk about it.
I move houses, Joanna visits Antwerp,
I purchase a sofa, she listens to Broken
Social Scene in the bath.
If she came over one evening
we'd climb out of the bathroom window
and drink wine on the roof.
The next day, we'd heat a pan of milk.
It would be a windy morning,
clouds racing across the skylight,
swallows hurtling around the block.
Joanna sitting on the floor
in her very soft white jumper
telling me about her sisters.
Everything would be clean.
The future would feel like rain on a golf umbrella
that we'd take turns holding.

Luke Samuel Yates

Introduction

Wellbeing is central to my work as an acupuncturist, requiring that attention is given to body, mind and spirit in the present moment. It encompasses the idea that our connections with other people, the world and its creatures are made in a spirit of kindness and generosity.

Attending to our wellbeing means being mindfully engaged in the creation of our own fulfilment. This departs from an idea that seems to hold great sway in contemporary times; the pursuit of happiness can overlook the fact that struggle is normal, expected and integral to human life.

Laurie Bolger's poem 'Yoga' honours close friendship; its quiet intimacy and its laughter. In 'Symbiosis' Em Gray describes seeing a horse lifting a dog in its mouth. Her tender poem touched me deeply. In 'Cardiologist' Jerrold Yam describes the solace found in the presence and attention of others when one's physical health is a concern. By committing to nurturing our wellbeing, we can access something greater than personal happiness. We can learn to subordinate our own demands to the needs of others, wherein lies the essence of love.

Poems are perfect vessels for holding emotional complexity and also for joyful celebration. As writer and reader, I am often delighted by how playful a poem can be. In Luke Yates' poem 'Swallows', the details of a relationship between lovers is imagined. A poem can return us to a child-self where stories are made and anything might happen.

Whilst they were written across three centuries the poems in this collection have much in common. Themes of friendship, family, the body in sickness and health, the natural world and its creatures are all here. Love, the work of the heart, in many forms underpins everything. May you find something you love in these pages.

Vanessa Lampert

Contents

		Page
Introduction	*Vanessa Lampert*	*5*
Swallows	*Luke Samuel Yates*	*7*
Meditations in an Emergency	*Cameron Awkward-Rich*	*8*
The Way Water Shapes a Landscape	*Paula Jennings*	*9*
Yoga	*Laurie Bolger*	*10*
Cardiologist	*Jerrold Yam*	*11*
Delphiniums in a Window Box	*Dean Young*	*12*
Symbiosis	*Em Gray*	*13*
Wood Song	*Sara Teasdale*	*14*
Great Things Have Happened	*Alden Nowlan*	*15*
Home	*Vanessa Lampert*	*16*

Published by:
Candlestick Press,
Diversity House, 72 Nottingham Road, Arnold, Nottingham NG5 6LF, UK
www.candlestickpress.co.uk

Design and typesetting by Craig Twigg

Printed by Bayliss Printing Company Ltd of Worksop, UK

Selection and Introduction © Vanessa Lampert, 2025

Cover illustration © Sara Boccaccini Meadows, 2025
https://www.boccaccinimeadows.com

Candlestick Press monogram © Barbara Shaw, 2008

© Candlestick Press, 2025

ISBN 978 1 913627 49 2

Acknowledgements

The poems in this pamphlet are reprinted from the following books, all by permission of the publishers listed unless stated otherwise. Every effort has been made to trace the copyright holders of the poems published in this book. The editor and publisher apologise if any material has been included without permission, or without the appropriate acknowledgement, and would be glad to be told of anyone who has not been consulted.

Thanks are due to all the copyright holders cited below for their kind permission.

Cameron Awkward-Rich, *Dispatch* (Persea Books, 2019) Copyright © 2019 by Cameron Awkward-Rich. Used by permission of Persea Books, Inc (New York), www.perseabooks.com. All rights reserved. Laurie Bolger, *Spin* (Smith|Doorstop, 2024). Em Gray, poem was originally published in *Mslexia* magazine, www.mslexia.co.uk Issue 97, March 2023 used with kind permission from the author. Paula Jennings, *This is You, Dear Stranger* (Red Squirrel Press, 2024) by kind permission of the Estate of Paula Jennings. Vanessa Lampert, poem was first published in this anthology. Alden Nowlan, *Between Tears and Laughter: Selected Poems* (Bloodaxe Books, 2004) www.bloodaxebooks.com. Jerrold Yam, *Intruder* (Ethos Books, 2014 and 2024) by kind permission of the author. Luke Samuel Yates, *Poetry Wales, Vol 56, issue 1*, by kind permission of the poet. Dean Young, *Fall Higher* (Copper Canyon Press, 2011) Copyright © 2011 by Dean Young. Reprinted by permission of The Permissions Company, LLC on behalf of Copper Canyon Press, www.coppercanyonpress.org.

All permissions cleared courtesy of Dr Suzanne Fairless-Aitken – Swift Permissions swiftpermissions@gmail.com.

Where poets are no longer living, their dates are given.

Ten Poems
for Wellbeing

Candlestick Press